# DANIEL ROTHAMEL

## Sidelines

*Finding success where coaches and referees meet*

Ben,

who would have ever thought that we would go from RETSO to this? Ha!
I am glad to be able to call you a friend and even moreso to call you a Brother in Christ.
Thank you for your friendship and support!

— Daniel

*This book was professionally typeset on Reedsy.*
*Find out more at reedsy.com*

*This book is dedicated to my wife, Kari. Without her sacrifice, love, and support, none of this would have been possible. She is living proof of the grace of God in my life.*

# Contents

*Introduction*                                                          iv

  *Let's go!*                                                  vii

1  Getting to Know You                                          1

  Coaches and officials are helpers at heart                    3

  The apple and the tree                                        4

  Why is this important?                                        4

  For the love of the game                                      5

  Why I became a referee                                        7

  To do our best                                                8

  How can we tell officials want to do their best?              9

  Working together for our collective best                      10

  A word about jerkfaces                                        11

  The wrap-up                                                   12

2  What Officials Really Want                                   13

  The philosophy of every official                             13

  What is preventive officiating?                              14

  You are already being preventive                             14

  Preventive officiating on the court/field                    15

  Samford's Law                                                 17

  The goal of every official                                    18

  The officials are trying to screw us                          19

  The wrap-up                                                   20

3  A Winning Game Plan                                          22

  Creating a winning game plan                                  23

  This is how you win                                           24

  Getting the official that you want                            25

How do I get officials who want to be there? 26

A game plan in three phases 27

The wrap-up 28

4 Pre-Game 30

For better or worse 31

The pre-game goal 32

A simple rule to follow 32

Handle your business 33

But wait, what about... 34

How to handle adverse situations 38

The same rule still applies 39

Why it matters 43

Knowing we've screwed up and learning from it 44

The wrap-up 44

5 In-Game 46

Perfection is the goal 47

How can this be perfection? 47

Interaction is distraction 48

Is perfection even possible? 48

The killer tactic 49

Implementing the killer tactic 51

How to interact, when you must 55

The wrap-up 59

6 Post-Game 61

Minimal interaction but opportunity for reinforcement 62

Locker room talk? 64

Interviews 65

Get it off your chest 66

Time for evaluation 67

Prepare wisely 68

The wrap-up 69

7 When Officials Screw Up 71

The three types of mistakes 72

On being evaluated                                    73

When mistakes are serious                             74

My first college game                                 75

A tale of two reactions                               77

The night I put sh*t in the game                      78

The breakdown and the lessons                         82

Addressing the mistakes officials make                85

The wrap-up                                           87

8   Respect and Reputation                            90

How did I get these officials?                        91

Keeping the bosses happy                              94

Follow the game plan all the way through              96

9   Ready for Success                                 97

10   We need Officials. You can Help.                 100

How do we get more officials?                         101

We must work together                                 102

# Introduction

Thank you.

I sincerely mean that. Thank you for reading this book. I know that there are a lot of other things that you could be doing right now, but you chose to read this book, and that means a lot to me. I promise you that I will do my best to make this time rewarding for you as a coach.

My name is Daniel Rothamel. I've spent a lot of time on the sidelines as a referee. I wrote this book, and it represents the experience that I've gained interacting with, and listening to, countless coaches countless times over the course of my officiating career. I've been officiating sports since I was sixteen. Most recently, I spent eighteen seasons officiating basketball at the high school level, including eight seasons officiating NCAA men's basketball at the D3 level.

My goal with this book is to use my experience as a referee to help you as a coach. That might seem a little bit odd to you, but this introduction will lay out exactly how I plan to do that, and how you can benefit from reading this book.

## Who is this book for?

The simple answer is—you. I'm writing this book to help you and coaches just like you.

- If you are the kind of coach who loves to learn new skills and tactics to improve your coaching—this book is for you.
- If you are the kind of coach who has experienced frustration with officials,

but you don't know exactly how to fix it—this book is for you.
- If you are the kind of coach who cares about the athletes and creating a positive experience for them—this book is for you.
- If you are the kind of coach who knows that there are probably things you could learn about officials that could help you—this book is for you.

This book isn't just for coaches, though. If you are a tournament director, league official, or school administrator, this book is also for you, because it will help you help your coaches. You can help the coaches you work with by passing on to them some of the things you learn in this book. You can also use what you learn to create a positive environment in your respective programs or leagues.

I designed this book so that it will be as accessible as possible to coaches of almost any sport at almost every level of coaching. There is something that every coach can learn from this book.

## Why should you care?

The content of this book is important because coaches and officials have to interact and work together. In my experience as a trainer, educator, and rules interpreter for officials, the officials spend a lot of time thinking about, preparing for, and training for their interactions with coaches. On the flipside, coaches don't usually get much training on how to interact with officials in a way that can truly benefit them and the officials. Coaches and officials have to work together, but they don't often cooperate. I think that we can, and should, change that, because coaches and officials often have many of the same goals and motivations.

From a purely competitive standpoint for you as a coach, reading this book will give you an advantage over many of your opponents who haven't read it. By reading this book, you are going to become the kind of coach that officials want to work for, and that administrators and league directors want to work with. While your colleagues remain frustrated by the officials, which affects their interaction with officials negatively, you'll be able to interact with officials frustration-free, positively impacting your interaction with officials. Less frustration means that you'll be spending more time coaching, while your opponent is distracted by their frustration with officials.

## What will you learn?

Overall, you're going to learn how you can create and maintain a positive environment that will lead to a positive relationship with game officials. But more specifically:

- You'll learn what motivates officials and how they are a lot like you.
- You'll learn what officials really want from every game they officiate.
- You'll learn about the philosophy that guides every official, and how you can use that philosophy to your advantage.
- You'll learn Samford's Law.
- You'll learn the importance of having a game plan when you deal with the officials and how you can use it to win with them.
- You'll learn what to do pre-game to set yourself up for success with the officials.
- You'll learn how to interact with officials during the game to help you get what you want.
- You'll learn how to use the post-game time to reinforce your commitment to a positive relationship with officials.
- You'll learn how to handle those situations when officials screw up in a way that will be good for you and the officials.
- You'll learn how all of this works together to help you earn the respect of game officials, administrators, and league directors so that your reputation will improve.

You'll learn many more tactics and strategies as well, but even if you only remember the ones on this list, you'll be a better coach for it.

## How will you learn?

I'm going to be sharing from my own experience, along with what I've learned from the experiences of others. In officiating, every official stands on the shoulders of those who have come before, and I've had the privilege of standing on some very strong shoulders. I want to use what I've learned to help you.

I'm also going to be sharing specific examples from my own career on the court. Since these are personal examples, they will all come from basketball. But that doesn't mean that you can't learn from them if you aren't a basketball coach. The lessons that I'm going to share will be valuable to you, no matter what sport you are coaching.

My writing style here is the same style I use when I am training and educating officials: direct. I don't want to waste your time. I want to make sure that I get you the information that you need, in a way that you can easily understand, so that you can apply it in your own work as quickly and effectively as possible.


## Let's go!

I hope that this brief introduction has given you a good idea of what to expect from reading the rest of this book. I also hope I've made you excited to get started, motivated to learn, and determined to apply what you're going to learn, because I'm excited to share this information with you...

# 1

# Getting to Know You

*"A common mistake among those who work in sport is spending a disproportional amount of time on "X's and O's" as compared to time spent learning about people."*
—*Mike Krzyzewski*

Ask yourself this question: *Outside of actual games, how much have you ever really thought about officials?*

The answer is probably not much. *And that's okay.*

As a coach, you have many responsibilities to fulfill and tasks to get done. All of that preparation requires a lot of your time and attention, on top of all of your obligations outside of your coaching. It's entirely understandable that coaches don't spend a whole lot of time thinking about the officials. But I want to ask you another question:

*If you spent a little time thinking about officials, how might it impact your coaching?*

I believe that if you take a little bit of time to consider officials and their role in what you do as a coach, you'll find that the little bit of time you spend will have significant positive impact on your coaching.

The fact is that there is a knowledge gap in sports when it comes to officials.

The officials are an integral part of every game, but the vast majority of people in sports don't know much about them, what motivates them, or how they do what they do.

Part of that is by design. Officials work very hard to go unnoticed. If you ask any official in any sport how they know if they've done a good job in a game, you'll likely hear an answer like, "If no one notices me, then I'm doing a good job."

The problem is that that lack of knowledge can also create misunderstanding, and that misunderstanding can lead to negative relationships between officials and the people they need to work with, especially coaches.

In this chapter, I'm going to challenge you to think about officials in ways that you might never have thought about them before. I'm going to lead you through this thought process so that you can have a greater understanding of the men and women who officiate your games, which will lead you to having better relationships with those men and women, which will improve your in-game experiences, and ultimately, make you a better coach.

Together, we're going to examine the core motivations for why officials do what they do, and compare them with your core motivations for coaching. I think you're going to find that you and your fellow coaches have a lot more in common with officials than you might expect. Specifically, I think that the core motivations of officials and coaches are often the same. This means that coaches and officials share a common foundation that they can use to build positive relationships.

Because we are all unique people, there are almost as many core motivations as there are coaches and officials; but some motivations are more common and some are more important than others. I believe that there are three core motivations that coaches and officials share that can serve as the strong foundation for positive relationships:

1. Coaches and officials both love to help.
2. Coaches and officials both love the game.
3. Coaches and officials both want to do their best.

The amount of time required to be a successful coach or official is tremendous. It means that coaches and officials make significant sacrifices to do what they do. Every minute spent coaching or officiating is a minute that can't be spent with family and friends, or at work, or on hobbies.

Because of the sacrifice involved, the motivations of coaches and officials has to be very strong, and it has to be very valuable to them. I believe that the three points I've just outlined are so strong and valuable that they form the core of what motivates coaches and officials to do what they do.

Once we all recognize and acknowledge our common motivations, we will have a strong foundation on which to build positive relationships, which is good for all of us, the athletes, and the games.

In order to understand each other better and build that foundation, let's take a look at each of these core motivations more closely...

## Coaches and officials are helpers at heart

Every official, just like every coach, has their own unique story about how and why they started on their particular path. After hearing countless examples of such stories from other officials and coaches, I've noticed a common theme that forms the first block in our foundation: coaches and officials love to help.

When officials have a job outside of officiating, or if they had a career before they started officiating, these careers usually fall into what I would call the "helper" category. Many officials are or were police officers, members of the military, teachers, etc. For the ones that aren't (or weren't), they often come from other fields that are oriented toward helping people: real estate agents (as I was), customer service professionals, HR professionals, entrepreneurs, etc.

You might be tempted to think that the reason this is true is because these jobs all offer a degree of flexibility that allows these men and women the time to officiate games. While that is partially true, I think the real reason that so many officials come from these kids of "helper" backgrounds is because most officials are motivated by helping others. Officiating allows them to apply that motivation to the sports that they enjoy.

Now think about coaches. Most of the coaches that I have known have similar backgrounds to officials. They usually have had some kind of "helper" job. Coaches that work in high school athletics are often teachers, and many of the ones that aren't come from the same types of jobs that I mentioned above.

Fundamentally, coaches and officials are helpers. They love to help other people, and they use this as motivation to help the kids that they either coach or officiate.

Does this apply to you? Because it definitely applies to me.

## The apple and the tree

It might be easy to look at my background and say that it is unique to me, and doesn't really mean anything to the wider worlds of coaching and officiating. But then, you'd also have to consider my family.

My dad was a USSSA softball umpire for many years, and I have fond memories of spending more than a few evenings and weekends at various softball fields around Long Island, New York, watching my dad with my mom. I spent a lot of time watching my dad with my face pressed to chain-link fences, and picking bleacher splinters from my hands and legs (yes, I'm old enough to remember when aluminum bleachers were a luxury most fields didn't have).

While my dad was an umpire, he was also something else: a teacher and a coach. He taught phys. ed. and coached high school basketball and soccer. My dad fit perfectly into the mold of a helper and teacher who applied that motivation to sports to become both a coach *and* an official.

## Why is this important?

I'm sharing this little bit of officiating origin about me and my dad in the hope that it resonates with your own origin story as a coach. I've got a hunch it probably does.

I know that neither he nor I am alone. The mold of helper who becomes official is a well-worn one, and so is the mold of the helper who becomes coach. Sometimes, that mold creates people, like my dad, who have done both.

I'm willing to bet this is exactly the mold from which you have been formed into the coach you are today. I'm hoping that you'll now be able to recognize the marks of that mold on the officials who are going to be working your games. I've met literally thousands of coaches and fellow officials during my career, and the vast majority of them share very similar circumstances: they share a theme of wanting to help others learn and grow.

What I hope that you'll take away from this is that the next time you arrive at your game and see the officials approaching, remember that they're doing what they're doing for many of the same reasons that you're doing what you're doing. You both want to help others learn and grown through sports. You both come from the same mold, and you can use what you share in common to help each other and the athletes that you care for.

Yes, the mold that made you into the coach you are today is shared by the officials who work your games, but that's not the only thing you share...

## For the love of the game

In my experience, it is extremely rare that an official or coach is involved with a sport with which they have no prior experience or knowledge. When you think about it, this makes total sense. People are always going to gravitate toward being involved in the sports with which they have experience, or at least interest.

I got started in basketball officiating because I had played basketball in high school. My dad had also been a high school basketball coach when I was young, so my exposure and experience with basketball had been significant.

Many other officials and coaches I have known played the sports that they officiate, at least on some level. Some played as kids, some played in high school, and some played in college or even professionally. But after their playing days ended, they were looking for a way to stay close to their sport—and because they also liked to help people, they eventually found officiating or coaching as a way to combine those two interests.

That brings us to our second key motivator that coaches and officials share in common: *love for the game.*

This love for the game manifests itself in many ways for coaches and officials, but the best way it does so is in commitment and dedication. The men and women who officiate, along with those who coach, are committed and dedicated to what they do in a way that often confounds people who can't understand why someone would spend so much time and effort to do something for which there is only a small financial reward.

After all, no one is getting rich being a high school or recreational coach or official, but that doesn't mean it isn't incredibly rewarding. The true reward comes in satisfying the love that coaches and officials have for their games and players. That's a major reason why we remain committed to doing what we do.

When you're coaching, I can guarantee you that whenever officials show up to your games, those officials love the game that they're officiating, and they love helping the kids who are playing it. If they didn't, they wouldn't show up.

I know this because I have been one of those officials. I have been one of the officials who had to travel hours to a game, leaving work early, leaving family and friends behind, to work a game that few people would watch, and even fewer would ever talk about. I was actually traveling home from a game on the night my wife went into labor with our first child. (During the game, I kept my cell phone at the scorer's table and told the PA announcer that if the caller ID flashed, "MY WIFE," he needed to give me a signal.)

I did all that traveling and spent all of that time because I love the game, and I want to be part of it. The reward for me wasn't financial, even though I was being paid; the reward was in knowing that I had done what I could to create a positive experience for everyone involved in my games.

Among officials, especially at the lower levels of officiating, you will hear a common saying: "You do it for the love, but you cash the checks."

Every sports official knows that, in order to be able to continue with officiating, you have to do it for something that is greater than the financial reward. For every official, the love of the game is a reward in and of itself.

When I was officiating, I knew that every coach I worked for shared a similar love. I knew that they had made tremendous unseen sacrifices to be in that gym with me and their players for that game. I knew that they were dedicated to the game and the players that they coached.

And that's where we can use our shared love for the game to build a foundation for positive relationships. The first step in making that positive impact is recognizing and acknowledging that we, as coaches and officials, share a love for the game that makes us committed to the best possible experience for the players and everyone else involved.

The next step is being committed to doing our best...

## Why I became a referee

I want to share a little bit about how and why I became an official, because I think it illustrates our point about the love of helping others being a motivation coaches and officials hold in common.

The first game that I ever officiated, of any kind, was a Dixie Youth baseball game in my hometown. I was fifteen. I was pressed into service because our local league desperately needed umpires, the guy who ran the league knew that I was on the varsity baseball team at the time, and he also knew that my Dad was a former USSSA softball umpire. He asked me if I would like to make a little bit of money umpiring games, and as a fifteen-year-old kid, there was no way I was going to turn down a few extra bucks. In short, the league needed help, and when they asked, I helped.

That experience led me to other opportunities to officiate rec-league sports in my rural Virginia county. During high school, I officiated baseball, softball, and soccer whenever I was available. I enjoyed it very much, and it all started because someone asked me to help fill their umpire void.

A few months into my first semester of college, I saw a flyer posted in the student center on campus. It was from the campus recreation department, and it said they needed help officiating intramural sports. Basketball was starting up, and I had played basketball in high school, so it seemed like a perfect fit. Officiating basketball led to officiating softball, which led to officiating flag football and basically anything else I could make time for. But it all started because the campus recreation department put out a call for help. As someone who likes to help, I was a moth to the flame.

While I was officiating intramural sports, I was also something else: an education major. So I was training to be both an official and a schoolteacher; and while I would never actually become a schoolteacher after graduation, I did continue officiating for almost two decades. I don't think that my inclinations toward helping, teaching, and officiating were coincidental, either.

## To do our best

By this point, I hope that you're able to recognize that officials and coaches are all motivated by a desire to help and a love for the game. Once we recognize the third motivation that coaches and officials share, we'll have a strong foundation on which to build a positive relationship that can benefit everyone involved.

The third motivation is *to do our best.*

I already know that you want to do your best, because you're reading this book. Reading this book is a signal that you want to grow, learn, and improve. It's a signal that you are motivated to do your best.

From the outside, most people evaluate how dedicated a coach is to doing their best by a win/loss record, but coaches know better. You know that there are a lot of things that you do that don't show up on the stat sheet; you know that winning is important, but there are times when it isn't as important as taking care of your players and putting them on the path to growing and developing into the best young men and women they can be. You know that twenty years from now, the players that you've touched will talk less about wins and losses and more about the lessons that they learned from you—lessons that they continue to value and pass on to others.

It is your commitment to doing your best for your players that helps them do their best as athletes, students, and people.

And when you've fallen short, and haven't done your best, you know it. It eats at you. I'm sure that you are haunted by decisions that you've made or actions that you've taken that didn't reflect your best to your athletes. But you use those experiences as learning opportunities so that you can improve and make your best even better.

For coaches, while some of the results aren't as obvious as others, the commitment to doing your best is visible; for officials, it can sometimes be harder to see the commitment, but you can rest assured that it is just as strong.

## How can we tell officials want to do their best?

Officials never win or lose any games. There is no public record to be evaluated, and they don't have players with whom they spend time teaching and developing, so there is often very little record of their accomplishments, if any at all.

This is another one of those aspects of officiating that is this way by design, and it goes back to what I mentioned earlier about officials not wanting to be noticed. The nature of officiating is that there is very little opportunity for the public to evaluate how successful officials are at what they do. Ask someone, even a fellow coach, how they would define the "best" official, and you're likely to get many, many different answers.

But just because it is hard for the public to define what goes into an official doing his or her best doesn't mean that officials can't define it.

There are a few popular sayings among officials that illustrate this point—

*"Officiating is one of the only things you can do where you are expected to be perfect, and then get better."*

*"There is no such thing as calling the perfect game."*

*"Do your best in every game, and work on getting better in every game."*

In my experience officials embrace the truth of each of these statements in succession, over time. They begin by wanting to be perfect and thinking that they can get every single call right, every single play right, every single mechanic right. This usually lasts for a couple games, and then it becomes very apparent that perfection is an impossible goal. Accepting that fact is key to an official's longevity, because it forces them to adopt the philosophy expressed by the third statement. The best officials I've known all swear by that philosophy, and they'll practice it until the day that they retire.

It's a sort of paradox: officials are committed to doing their best when they are committed to doing better each time.

Getting better as an official is something that always drives officials. Officials spend a lot of time and money learning about officiating and especially going to camps to learn from their colleagues and get better during the off-season.

Aside from being helpers, which we've already looked at, a lot of officials are driven by the fact that officiating is something at which they can always improve, and always learn something new. Officiating is many things, but it is never boring.

Part of what fends off potential boredom is the commitment that officials have to doing their best in every game, which means they are always looking for things they can learn from their games so that they can get better for the next game.

While it might be hard for the public to determine criteria for evaluating whether or not an official is doing their best, I can guarantee that every official has their own criteria, and they know exactly where they stand, all the time.

And just like coaches, every official knows the times when they weren't at their best, and those times stick with them forever. I know I have plenty of those stories (some of which I'll share later), but every official uses each of those times as a learning opportunity so that they can improve and make their best even better.

## Working together for our collective best

Coaches and officials all want to do their best. They want to do their best for themselves and for the players and participants in their games. Recognizing and acknowledging this shared motivation to doing their best is something that coaches and officials can use as a foundation to build more positive relationships because it is a shared commitment that positively impacts each other and everyone involved in sports.

When coaches and officials are able to recognize and acknowledge this shared motivation, they are able to encourage each other and feed this motivation. Later on in this book, I'll share some of the simple, practical ways that you can do this as a coach. Once you do, it will have a positive impact on your experience with officials.

## A word about jerkfaces

I realize that you might have read this and thought to yourself, "this sounds great, Daniel, but there are some officials out there who aren't like this. They don't seem to care, or they only care about themselves."

The truth is—you're right.

Officials aren't perfect, and there are most certainly officials out there who don't possess the characteristics I've described. I know because I've met them and even worked with them. I call them jerkfaces. (There might be various other less polite things that people call them.)

One thing I've always said is that survival in officiating requires a healthy ego. Without one, an official simply won't last. Some people are able to control their ego, others are not as good at controlling it.

If you're being honest, you probably know similar people within the coaching ranks. I'm sure that doesn't prevent you from doing your job to the best of your ability and doing it the right way. The same is true of officials. What I want to do is help you to see the commonalities you have with the vast majority of officials because that will help you recognize the best officials out there, and once you recognize them, they'll recognize you. Together, you can transform the relationship between coaches and officials for the better.

I will also say that, during my eighteen seasons of officiating high school and NCAA basketball, the number of jerkfaces has been drastically reduced. People have a natural inclination away from jerkfaces, and that includes officiating supervisors and assignors.

Are there jerkfaces in officiating? Yes.

Can we reduce their number by encouraging the good officials and strengthening those relationships? Also yes.

Let's do that.

## The wrap-up

Our goal for this chapter was to lay a strong foundation on which coaches and officials can build positive relationships. That foundation is the three major motivations that coaches and officials share:

1. Coaches and officials both love to help.
2. Coaches and officials both love the game.
3. Coaches and officials both want to do their best.

Recognizing these shared motivations and being willing to acknowledge them in each other will form the foundation for positive relationships between you and the officials in your games.

Once you can understand that officials love to help (just as you do), and that officials love the game (just as you do), and that officials want to do their best (just as you do), you'll be ready to work *with* them, using those shared motivations to have a positive impact on each other and the game.

Now that we've explored the motivations of officials as a common foundation, I want to take you further inside the mind of officials and share with you the main goal that *every official has for every game that they officiate.*

You've done a great job being open to learning about the motivations of officials, but once you understand the goal of officials, you'll be able to to pair your shared motivations with their goal to transform your relationship with officials, which will impact your coaching in a positive way.

# 2

# What Officials Really Want

*"The objective of a referee is not to get mentioned. I tell a lot of young referees that not being mentioned is king. If you can achieve that, that then it has been a pretty good game."*
   —*Alan Lewis (international rugby referee)*

Now that you are able to understand the core motivations for why officials choose to become officials, it's time to pair that information with the key goal of every official in every game. Once you know both the motivations and the goal of all officials, you'll be able to integrate them with your own motivations and goals and start building relationships with them so you can work toward a common goal.

## The philosophy of every official

As with coaching, there are fundamentals for officiating that every official has to learn. Aside from the rules of the games that they officiate, officials have to learn about the principles and mechanics that are part of what they do. These principles and mechanics are unique to every sport, but there is a particular philosophy of officiating that is universal and adhered to by every official: *preventive officiating.*

Understanding preventive officiating will help you understand the goal of officials in their games, and why they take many of the actions that they take during a game.

## What is preventive officiating?

It is possible to write an entire separate book on preventive officiating, but that would be a book for officials, not for coaches like you. For you, I just want to introduce you to the philosophy so that you can understand how it guides the actions that officials take (or don't take), and how it affects your games and what you do as a coach. With this understanding, you can work better with officials (and I'll give you plenty of practical tips on how to do exactly that in the upcoming chapters).

Let's start with a definition of preventive officiating:

**Preventive officiating is the philosophy that officials should do everything they can to prevent problems \*before\* they occur.**

Let's look at two examples that will help you understand preventive officiating—one that has nothing to do with sports, and another from actual games.

## You are already being preventive

You probably own a vehicle. You know that one of the biggest potential expenses on your vehicle is maintenance. When something goes wrong, getting it fixed costs you extra money—sometimes a lot of it. Even when you know how to fix the problem yourself, you have to spend time and money that you didn't anticipate spending to make the problem go away.

To prevent these problems, you (hopefully) perform "preventive maintenance" on your vehicle. That means that you do things like changing the oil regularly, checking the air pressure on your tires and making sure they are properly filled, washing your vehicle to protect the paint and finishes from dirt and rust, etc.

All of those preventive actions are taken so that you can avoid problems with your vehicle. For example, if you didn't take the preventive action of changing the oil, you could severely damage your engine and cost yourself thousands of dollars. If you don't keep your tires properly inflated, they will wear out more quickly, or even fail suddenly, potentially leading to a serious accident.

Preventive officiating works in the exact same way. Officials take specific actions so that they can prevent as many problems as possible from arising during the course of a game. They take small actions to avoid having to take more serious actions later on.

Just as with the preventive maintenance you take on your vehicle, there is no way to prevent one hundred percent of all possible problems, because there is always the possibility of unexpected incidents, like an accident or a sudden part failure. But your preventive maintenance greatly reduces the amount of fixing that you have to do on your vehicle, and it makes your ownership experience much more enjoyable and less expensive, overall.

The same is true of preventive officiating. Officials know that they cannot possibly prevent every single problem or adverse situation in their games. Players will often do unexpected things, and sometimes they fail to do the right things, and officials have to deal with those situations. But preventive officiating greatly reduces the amount of times officials need to take serious action, and it makes the game experience much more enjoyable for everyone involved.

Now that you can understand the idea of preventive officiating, let's take a look at how it impacts actual games...

## Preventive officiating on the court/field

Every game has three phases: pre-game, in-game, and post-game. We're going to learn about the unique importance of each of these phases soon, but I want to share simple examples of ways that preventive officiating is applied in each of these phases.

## Pre-game:

During warm-ups, officials notice that a player has a piece of gear that violates the rules. If the official allows the game to begin with the illegal gear present, they will have to penalize the player, and the player's team. Instead of allowing the problem to arise during the game, preventive officiating means that the official will go to the player and the player's coach and let them know what the violation is so that they can correct it before the game begins. This simple act of talking to the player and the coach prevents what could become a major problem in the game.

## In-game:

During the course of play, an official notices that a player is getting frustrated and is getting close to lashing out at an opponent, which could result in having to assess penalties, or—worse—a fight. Preventive officiating means that the official will try to diffuse the situation by going to the captain, a teammate, or a coach—and sometimes the player—to let them know what the official is seeing and ask them to help diffuse the situation. This helps prevent what could become a huge problem that would have a serious negative impact on the game.

## Post-game:

If you've ever wondered why game officials try to make a quick and direct exit the moment that a game is over, it's because they are being preventive officials. Almost every sport has rules about the jurisdiction of officials lasting beyond the end of the game, for as long as they are on the field/court (in basketball, it's "within the visual confines of the court"). One of the last things that officials want to do is have to administer penalties after a game has ended—it can make things rather messy. Officials try to prevent this by leaving as quickly as they can, before any potential conflict or problem might arise.

These are just three simple examples of how officials apply the philosophy of preventive officiating into everything that they do, in all phases of the game. I'm sure you can think of other examples that you've seen or experienced, even if you weren't aware that preventive officiating was behind them.

Preventive officiating is something that is drilled into every official, early and often throughout their career. I want to share an effective way I learned the value of preventive officiating that might be useful to you in your coaching, as well...

## Samford's Law

When I was selected for the men's basketball officiating staff of the USA South Athletic Conference, my supervisor was a man by the name of Wayne Samford.

Wayne is one of the most unique characters I've ever met—and one of the best officials I've ever met, as well. He had decades of NCAA experience by the time he became the supervisor of the USA South, and he exemplified all of the best attributes we've discussed here.

Wayne had a mantra that he drilled into the head of every official that ever worked with him. It was a mantra that he said he had developed early in his career, before the term "preventive officiating" had ever been used, but it was the mantra he used to explain the philosophy in an easy-to-grasp and memorable way. He ended every staff meeting with it; he used it in all his communications; it was the way he started and ended his pre-game meetings, and the last thing he said to his crew before they took to the court for the opening jump-ball. Wayne called it his mantra, but I call it "Samford's Law." It is very simple:

**DON'T PUT ANY SH\*T IN THE GAME.**

Every official knows exactly what this means when they hear it. They know that this is the essence of preventive officiating. In just a few words, Wayne distilled the entire philosophy of preventive officiating into this simple phrase. And it works.

At the core, preventive officiating is about preventing, and not creating, problems. Samford's Law expresses this perfectly. And just like any law, when you violate it, the consequences are swift and unpleasant. Every official has stories where they have violated Samford's law, and while those stories are great learning opportunities, and they might even be amusing in hindsight, I can assure you that living them isn't fun.

As helpful as this is to officials, I think it is probably applicable to you as a coach, too. If you coach in a way that prevents, and doesn't create, problems for you and your players, you'll likely find that the experience for everyone is vastly improved.

As we move through this book, I'll be referencing Samford's Law, how you can apply it in your interactions with officials, and how officials might apply it in their interactions with you, to move everyone toward a positive experience.

I learned a lot about how to be a basketball official from Wayne Samford, but it is his mantra—Samford's Law—that every official who ever met Wayne Samford remembers and carries with them. Wayne died in a tragic motorcycle accident in 2014, but his legacy in officiating lives on in the lives and careers of every official who has lived and worked by his mantra, by Samford's Law.

Now that you know what preventive officiating is, and you have Samford's Law to guide your understanding of it, let's take a look at how they both serve to meet the ultimate goal of every official in every game that they work.

## The goal of every official

I want you to think about a time when you were involved in a situation where you had to work with someone to achieve a win-win for both of you, even when it seemed like you had different objectives. Maybe it was working with your kids or your spouse to do something, or maybe it was negotiating the sale of a car with a dealership. Just think about how you were able to achieve a win-win outcome.

Achieving that win-win required you to know what the other person's goal was, along with how you could meet their goal while still meeting your goal. You probably didn't get everything exactly the way you wanted it, and they probably didn't either, but you both got something you wanted in the end.

Working with officials is a lot like that.

As a coach, you have a goal: to win the game. You probably have a lot of other goals within a game, too. You want to see your players perform in a particular way, or you have stats that you want to achieve, etc. You have to work with your players and the officials to achieve those goals, and hopefully to achieve your ultimate goal of winning.

Officials have a goal, too. And while it is impossible for officials to win or lose any game, and they each have their own individual goals for improvement within a game, there is one goal that every single official has for every single game that they work, and it's the reason that they apply Samford's Law and preventive officiating. Once you know and understand this goal, you'll be able to work with every official you come into contact with to achieve a win-win for both of you...

**_Officials want a game without any problems._**

That's it. That is the core goal of every official in every game. Everything they do, every action they take (or don't take) is in service to the goal of officiating the game without any problems.

Officiating is difficult enough without problems causing officials extra stress and work. Talk to any official, and they will tell you that they would love to work a game where they never had to call a technical foul, throw a flag, show a card, call a penalty, or dispute a call with a player or coach.

Once you understand that everything an official does is in an effort to prevent problems, every call they make is an effort to prevent making another call, every interaction is an effort to diffuse conflict that can lead to problems, you'll be well on your way to improving your relationship with officials.

## The officials are trying to screw us

I've watched a lot of sports from the fan perspective. I've heard a lot of discussions about officials from fans, players, and coaches. Being an official gives me a different perspective on games. Fans, players, and sometimes coaches will make a comment like "The officials are trying to screw us."—the idea being that the officials have a personal vendetta against a particular team, coach, or player that they enforce through their officiating.

I can tell you that it is possible that officials sometimes do this. Officials are human, and sometimes, some officials aren't ethical. It happens. But I would be willing to peg the instances of an official intentionally doing something to hurt a team, coach, or player as very, very close to zero.

For what it's worth, I can promise you that officials don't care who wins or loses. Officials have so many other things to concern themselves with that who wins and loses isn't even on their radar. I think what people are usually expressing when they make a comment like this is that they don't understand why an official did, or didn't do, something. And because they don't understand it, they tend to assign a negative motive to it.

That's a major reason why I'm writing this book for you—to remove the misunderstanding. Instead of misunderstanding why officials do what they do, I want you to understand what motivates their actions. Understanding the actions of the officials helps you react to situations in a way that is better for you and your team. A better understanding of the actions of officials also goes a long way to alleviating the frustration you might sometimes feel, because everyone gets frustrated by things they can't understand or explain. Now, you have a framework to explain almost anything that an official does in a game.

## The wrap-up

It's important to keep in mind the things that you've learned in this chapter, because we'll be coming back to them throughout the rest of the book. Let's review briefly:

- The core philosophy of every official is preventive officiating.
- Samford's Law is an easy-to-remember way to practice preventive officiating.
- The goal of every official, in every game, is the same: a game without problems.

These key ideas guide the actions of every official, so understanding them is important. Once you understand why officials do what they do, you'll be able to respond to those actions in a way that will improve the relationship between you and the officials, rather than damaging it. Just as officials concentrate on preventive officiating, I'll share with you how you can do some preventive coaching to help generate a win-win for you and the officials that will lead to a better overall experience for everyone involved in your games.

In the next chapter, we're going to take a skill that you already have—game-planning—and put it to use with the officials. You'll see how creating an effective game plan for the officials can get you the results that you want.

# 3

# A Winning Game Plan

*"Winning is not a sometime thing; it's an all-time thing. You don't win once in a while, you don't do things right once in a while, you do them right all the time. Winning is habit. Unfortunately, so is losing."*
*—Vince Lombardi*

As a coach, you have a lot of responsibilities to fulfill and skills to learn. Much like officiating, there is always something new to learn so that you can be a better coach. Because there is so much to learn, you have to prioritize some skills over other skills. You start with fundamentals, and then work your way up from there.

With so much to learn, it makes sense that "how to interact with officials" isn't super high on the list of skills to develop for most coaches. That's a major reason why I wrote this book, and you're already ahead of your competition by reading it. What we've covered so far is mostly philosophical, but now it's time to start getting practical.

As a coach, you have your own philosophy of how to coach and how to manage your players and the game. That philosophy forms the foundation for how you implement all of your tactical decisions—from your practice schedules to post-game meetings, and everything in between.

I'm sure that a significant portion of your time and attention is given to the game plan. As the old saying goes, if you fail to plan, you're planning to fail. Because you know this, you develop a game plan for each game, and then you give it to your players to execute.

We're going to apply this same strategy to your interactions with officials. You are already creating a game plan for every game, and I'm going to share with you how you can have a game plan for the officials that will complement any game plan you develop for your players.

If you're thinking that the last thing you need is one more to-do for each game, don't worry. This game plan for interacting with officials is going to be simple, straightforward, and won't have to change much from game to game. Once you understand how this game plan works, you'll be able to repeat it in every game while hardly giving it any thought at all. In other words, a little attention to it in the beginning is going to pay huge dividends for the rest of your coaching career.

This is probably going to be the shortest chapter of this book, but it's also one of the most important, so let's get to work and get a game plan going...

## Creating a winning game plan

Every game plan has a goal. I'm going to guess that, for you, all of your game plans are created with the same ultimate goal in mind: winning.

But this game plan is going to be different, because this is your game plan for interacting with the officials. Nobody is keeping score on your interactions with officials, but that doesn't mean that your game plan doesn't have a goal. It just means that we need to define the goal so that you can keep score. If the goal of your team's game plan is to win, we need to define what a "win" is going to look like in your game plan for the officials.

Earlier, I told you what every official wants from every game that they officiate—*no problems*. That's how officials define a "win." But what about you? How do *you* "win" with the officials?

Let me tell you what I've been told by countless coaches over the years, and what coach evaluations of officials say they want from officials in their games:

consistency.

Does that ring true to you? It should. You just want consistency from the officials. You want to know what to expect, so that you can coach your players on what to expect.

*You'll know you've had a win when you are getting better consistency from the officials in your games.*

## This is how you win

But here's the thing: officials already know that you want consistency your games. In fact, a huge part of the evaluation criteria of every official *is* their consistency. Consistency is something that gets drilled into the head of every official early and often.

That raises the question: *Why don't officials deliver consistency more frequently?*

That's a fair question, and there a few reasons that work together to explain inconsistency.

The first reason is that officials are human, and they make mistakes. The next reason is that officiating is part science, and part art. The science comes from knowing the rules of the game and the mechanics of officiating; the art comes from knowing when and how to apply and enforce the rules (the simple term for this is "judgment"). Inconsistency arises when officials fail at one of those two things. Either they mess up a rule or a mechanic, or they exercise poor judgment.

We've already established that it is likely impossible that any official will ever have a game where they make one hundred percent of the calls correctly. And if you work in a sport with multiple officials, you can just multiply that chance of imperfection exponentially.

We've also established that knowing the motivation of officials can help you improve your interactions with officials. In doing so, we've established that, just like you, officials always want to do the best job that they possibly can in every game. Now we know that this means that they want to be as consistent as they possibly can (as individuals and as a crew) in every game.

So how are you going to win and get better consistency out of the officials on your games?

*Officials are going to give you the most consistency when they are able to perform at their best. The easiest way for you to get more consistency from the officials on your game is to promote an environment that enables them to perform their best.*

It makes sense, right? When you have officials performing at their best, they are going to be at their most consistent. Aren't those the officials that you want on your games?

## Getting the official that you want

There's an old saying that you can pick your friends, but you can't pick your family. I'd apply something similar here and suggest that you can pick your players, but you can't pick your officials.

I'm sure that you're well aware of this. You likely had at least some say—maybe even total say—in who is on your roster. You chose these players for a lot of different reasons, but the main reason you chose each of them is because you felt they give you the best chance to win. After all, winning is the goal, right? But with the officials, you don't get to choose who does your games. You have to work with whoever shows up.

So, if you don't get to pick the officials who work your games, how do you get the officials that you want on your games? What kind of officials do you even want?

To answer that question, I want you to think back to something you've probably said as a coach when it comes to the players on your roster: you want the players who want to be there. You've probably said this when it came to a choice between a more talented player who wasn't committed to the team and a less-talented player who *was* committed. I'm guessing that you preferred the player who wanted to be there, and I think you were right.

This is exactly the type of official that you want on your games—you want the official who wants to be there. There might be more talented officials out there, or officials that you know better, but nothing beats the performance of an official who wants to be on that game. Trust me on this. I've worked thousands of games with hundreds of different officials all across the spectrum of officiating talent and experience. Any official who is focused and wants to be on a game beats an any official who is distracted or phoning it in, every single time.

## How do I get officials who want to be there?

The good news here is that every official has some degree of self-motivation. (Believe me, if you don't have self-motivation to officiate, you won't last long.) All you have to do is stoke the embers of that motivation into a fire.

Let's go back to the players I was just talking about. Think about a time you had a player that you knew had amazing potential, but for whatever reason, they were slacking on it. What did you do?

I'm guessing that you spent a little bit of time figuring out what motivated them, and then doing what you could to fuel that motivation.

You can't do exactly the same thing with officials, because you aren't around the officials all of the time, but you can definitely do some simple things to be successful with the exact same strategy.

The good news is that you have spent the beginning of this book learning what motivates officials. The best way you can support that motivation is by implementing a game plan to create the most positive environment you can.

Isn't that what you're already doing with your game-planning for your players? Your ultimate goal is to win, and you can best achieve that when you promote an environment that enables them to perform at their best. That's what your game plan is designed to do. Will you win every game? Nope. But your game plan will put you in a position to win.

Likewise, will you win every game when in comes to your interactions with officials? Nope. But by creating and implementing this game plan, you'll put yourself in a position to win, and you'll be able to make adjustments in the future.

Now, let's take a look at this plan...

# A game plan in three phases

Your game plan for interacting with officials is going to have three phases. Each of these phases is unique, each of them is important, and—building on what you've already learned about what motivates officials and their philosophy—each phase can be successfully executed with just a few simple tactics.

Here are the three phases of your game plan for interacting with officials:

1. Pre-game
2. In-game
3. Post-game

I told you this was simple and straightforward, right?

I'm going to devote a chapter to each of these phases and how to execute the plan for them in just a bit, but let's take a minute and look at a quick introduction to each phase.

## Pre-game

The pre-game phase of your game plan will cover everything that happens from the time you and the officials arrive at the game venue up to the start of the actual game.

It will cover the things that you can do to make sure you're setting yourself up for success before you even see the officials, all the way through how to handle introductions.

It will likely cover things you've never really given much thought to, but that are important to your game officials. Trust me on this—if you can nail your pre-game interactions with officials, it will go a LONG way toward creating a more positive in-game experience for you and your team.

## In-game

The in-game phase of your game plan will cover everything that happens from the start of the game until it is finished.

This is the phase that most coaches think about when they do think about interactions with officials. Building on the foundation that you will have built in the pre-game phase, you'll learn ways to approach your in-game interactions that will benefit you and your players.

There are a lot of complex dynamics at play during every game, and every game is unique, but we'll go over a variety of tactics you can apply that will make it easier for you to handle any situation that arises.

## Post-game

The post-game phase of the game plan will cover everything that happens after the game is over, until the next game begins.

The last thing you want to do is have successful pre-game and in-game phases, only to detract from them by doing something in the post-game that has an undesirable effect on future games.

Like the pre-game phase, this phase is probably going to include some things that you've never given much thought, but handling them with specific tactics can go a long way to future success.

# The wrap-up

The goal of your game plan for interacting with officials is to get the highest possible consistency out of the officials who work your games. This game plan is going to help you promote an environment that will enable the officials to perform at their best, and ensure that you have officials who want to be on your games, thereby giving you the most consistency possible.

The three phases of your game plan are simple:

1. Pre-game

2. In-game
3. Post-game

That's it. I told you this was going to be a short chapter. Now, let's look at each phase in more detail, and start creating some wins...

# 4

# Pre-Game

*"The key is not the will to win. Everybody has that. It is the will to prepare to win that is important."*
  *– Bobby Knight*

If you were an athlete of any kind, I want you to think back to when you used to compete. I want you to think specifically about how you prepared for games.

Chances are, you paid a lot of attention to what you did leading up to games. You tried to do the same things each time. You tried to eat the same things, at the same time, before each game. You tried to listen to the same music. You tried to warm-up the same way. You were trying to create a pre-game experience that would set you up for success in each game.

Now think about how you do this for your players. You do the same thing by trying to make their pre-game experience substantially the same for each game, because you know what it takes to create a positive pre-game experience that will set them up for success.

# For better or worse

Now I want you to think of a time when something disrupted that positive pregame experience that you worked so hard to create. Maybe the bus broke down on the way to the game. Maybe you couldn't have the food you wanted. Maybe you didn't get enough sleep. Maybe you forgot your favorite brace. Whatever it might have been, I want you think about how it affected your mindset going in to the game. It probably wasn't a positive effect, and you probably had to work a little harder than usual to overcome that negative start.

Now think about a time when everything went just as you planned it. Everything about your pre-game routine was just perfect. You got to the game with plenty of time to spare. Your pre-game meal was especially delicious. You were well-rested and had energy. Your uniform was clean and crisp when you walked out of the locker room. Whatever it was that made things perfect, I want you to think about how it affected your mindset going into the game. It probably made you feel like you could beat any opponent you were facing, and it probably made it easier to get going when the game started.

For better or worse, the pre-game experience lays the foundation for how we perform in the games. This is true for players, coaches, and also officials.

The goal of this chapter is to help you create a pre-game experience that is as positive as possible for your officials and your interactions with them. Because, for better or worse, the pre-game experience you create lays the foundation for the in-game experience.

Creating a positive pre-game experience for your officials will help them perform at their best; when you pair that with positive pre-game interactions, you're well on your way to having the best possible in-game experience with the officials. Creating a positive pre-game experience creates a positive in-game experience, which sets you up for success.

And with the officials, there are a lot of simple things you can do that have a huge positive impact on the pre-game experience.

## The pre-game goal

We've already established that the ultimate goal for your game plan for interacting with officials is to get the most possible consistency out of the officials on your games. That's your win.

But each phase of the game plan is going have its own goal that will build toward that goal of getting consistency from the officials. This is the goal of the pre-game phase of your game plan:

*The pre-game phase will lay a firm foundation for positive interactions with the officials, especially positive in-game interactions.*

You're going to learn some easy-to-implement strategies and tactics for achieving that goal of laying a firm foundation for positive interactions, and you'll see some examples of how those tactics work, and what happens when you don't use them.

## A simple rule to follow

Before we get into the specific strategies and tactics, I want to give you a simple rule you can follow that will guide you through all of your pre-game interactions with the officials:

**Be cordial at least, friendly at best, but always positive.**

When you don't know what to do, always refer back to this rule.

It is important to understand that officials are explicitly trained to put negative experiences behind them as quickly as possible and regain focus on the task at hand. It's part of the officials' job to do that. And while they are able to brush aside any sort of negative pre-game experience, the impact of a positive experience is much more powerful. A negative experience can be brushed aside, because that's part of what officials are trained to do, but a positive experience sticks with officials and makes it easier for them to do what they need to do to perform to the best of their abilities and deliver the consistency that you're looking for.

32

You don't have to be Mr. or Ms. Personality to do this. You just have to be committed to being as positive as you can. I know, things happen. Often, things beyond your control have an effect on how you interact at a game. That's life; officials know this, too. Interactions don't have to be perfect, but the more positive they can be, the better.

When you create a positive pre-game experience, you are creating a very strong foundation for the best possible in-game experience and putting yourself on the path to a win with the officials.

## Handle your business

One of the easiest and most important things you can do to create a positive pre-game experience is to make sure you're doing all of the things you're supposed to be doing. I know that sounds a little strange, but let me explain.

As a coach, you have your own pre-game responsibilities. Many of these responsibilities intersect with the the responsibilities of game officials. Here are some examples:

### Be prepared for the officials

When you are the host of a game, make sure that you are prepared for the officials. You probably know who the officials are, and you know that you should expect them to arrive thirty to sixty minutes before game time, at least, so doing what you can to make sure the officials are greeted by someone and shown to their facilities is a great way to put your best foot forward and show that you care about the pre-game experience.

I can tell you from experience that arriving at a venue and not having any clue what to do or where to go can be a frustrating experience. And while officials don't arrive to a venue expecting to be treated like a celebrity, the experience of simply being greeted by someone and shown to the facilities is a positive first impression that sticks with officials.

## Facilities

Think about the times that you've taken your team to away venues. You probably have in your mind the ones that have hospitable facilities, and the ones that don't, and it affects the way you go about your pre-game activities.

Officials do the exact same thing.

That means that you want to be as high on the list of hospitable facilities as possible, because it allows the officials to focus primarily on doing their jobs well, instead of planning to navigate the oddities of an inhospitable environment.

If you are the host of the game, you are responsible for providing the officials with a place where they can meet and get dressed. This might be a special locker room, or it might be an empty office or classroom. Regardless of what kind of space it is, you should try to do whatever you can to make that space a private one and as comfortable as possible for the officials. Make sure the space is clean and that the officials aren't going to come into contact with players, fans, or people other than game management personnel.

I'm not saying that you need to turn your officials' facilities into a five-star experience, but do whatever you can to make them as comfortable as possible. That little bit will go a long way.

## But wait, what about...

I can already tell what you're thinking—"this sounds great, Daniel, but what about all of those times when we play at a neutral venue, or a tournament, or we are the visiting team? We can't control these things for those games."

You're absolutely right. I know that. Officials know that, too. In the situation of neutral venues or when you're the visitor, you'll just have to trust in the venue and the tournament directors to handle their responsibilities with regard to the officials. Those things are out of your control when you play at a neutral site or when you are the visiting team.

Just because that is true, however, doesn't mean that there is nothing you can do to promote a positive pre-game experience. There are still a number of small ways you can have a major positive impact as a visiting team or at a neutral site, because they apply to every game, no matter where it is played.

## Equip your players properly

One thing you can do, that you already should be doing, is making sure that all of your players are properly equipped before they leave the locker room. Make sure everyone has all of their uniform pieces, and make sure that they aren't wearing anything that is illegal. If you know you need a medical exemption letter for something, make sure you have it.

I know that you don't like being the fashion police when it comes to uniforms, and the rules regarding acceptable uniform components seem to change every season, but uniform issues are one of the biggest headaches for officials, because they are entirely preventable (remember the principle of preventive officiating?), but uniform issues are best prevented by players and coaches, before officials have to deal with them.

Officials see a lot of crazy stuff when it comes to uniform rules, but I can tell you one thing that officials are seeing less and less of: a team that comes out of the locker room looking truly *uniform* and ready to play from the moment they step out of the locker room.

Having your team properly equipped when they leave the locker room is another way to make a major positive impression, while showing that you are working with the officials' philosophy of being preventive.

## Have your lineup ready

Every sport has a rule that determines how and when the final roster and lineup must be submitted to the game officials and approved.

I cannot stress this enough: FOLLOW THIS RULE. EVERY SINGLE GAME.

This particular rule is unique in every sport, and it can only be fulfilled by the coach, so you need to know exactly what it is, and you need to follow it for every single game.

I can tell you that a point of frustration for officials in every sport is the roster/lineup rule. It is ignored far too often.

Remember what I said about Samford's Law? Well, starting the game with a penalty or having to change the pre-game procedures because your team didn't follow the roster/lineup rule both violate the law. Failure to follow that rule puts sh*t in the game. Follow the rule.

If you are already following that rule every single game, that's awesome. Keep it up.

But be honest, and if you know that officials have been letting you slide on following the proper roster/lineup procedures, they're doing you a huge favor. Don't take advantage of them. Think about how you can make sure that you are always following the rule.

When you follow this rule, it shows the the officials that you are on top of your game and that you care about the rules. Like many of the other things we've already discussed, officials are able to brush aside a failure to follow the rule (even if they do have to assess a penalty for it), but if you are following it properly, you are ensuring a positive pre-game experience that will stick with officials.

## Pick a good captain

I'll admit that this is a controversial tip to be included, but I'm going to throw it in here for your consideration. Ignore it if you want, but I want you to at least consider it. If this doesn't apply to your sport, or if you coach at an age level where "captain" is more of a ceremonial title, feel free to skip ahead (or you can keep reading to see if maybe there is some way it might apply to you).

The rules of most sports dictate that each team needs a captain. The rules don't specify how that captain is to be selected; every team picks their captains differently. Maybe the players vote. Maybe you pick the captain(s). Maybe you change captain(s) from game to game. The criteria you have for picking captains is also unique to you and your team. That's the way it should be. I just want to make a small suggestion with regard to the captain(s) that you might want to consider.

Consider choosing a captain that can be an asset to the officials during the game. Here's why...

Part of preventive officiating for the officials is paying close attention to the personality and conduct of players during the game. Officials are trained to look for players who might get themselves and others in trouble, or cause trouble, and be aware of them. On the flip side, officials are also trained to look for players that they can rely upon to help manage those potentially problematic teammates or situations during a game.

Officials are trained this way because it is better for the game when problems can be prevented (remember the main goal of the officials?) and it is even better when the players can learn to prevent the problems. For this reason, officials will often communicate things to players that can help improve the game, and they rely on the players to help.

Obviously, the first player an official will look to will be the captain, because the assumption is that the captain has been chosen for their leadership ability, which includes maturity and levelheadedness. I want to suggest that you should look for those qualities in a captain.

It is certainly possible that the player on your team who might be best suited to interact with officials might not be a player who plays a lot. That's fine. It just means that, of the players who you know are going to play a lot, find one that the officials can talk to. See if you can make that player one of the captains. If you can't make that player the captain, that's okay, too.

When you have identified that player, let them know that you expect them to be the one that the officials can talk to, and have them notify the officials of the same. They don't have to make a big deal about it.

I can tell you that it is a big relief for the officials when a player comes to them and simply says, "Hey, if y'all need anything from my teammates, you can let me know. I can help talk to them."

The officials may or may not ever talk with that player, but they will appreciate knowing who they can rely on, and it will make a powerful positive impression.

## The pre-game greeting

Before any of your games begins, there is always a moment when you will have to greet and introduce yourself to the game officials. This is another simple opportunity to create a positive experience and leave a positive impression.

Let's go back to what I said earlier in this chapter regarding your pre-game interactions with officials: be cordial at least, friendly at best, but always positive.

The pre-game greeting of officials is the perfect time to put this into practice. You should greet the officials with a firm handshake (or fist bump, nowadays) good eye contact, and a positive greeting. If you don't know the officials, tell them your full name.

You can also finish off with a simple "Good luck tonight," or something similar. You don't have to engage in a long conversation with the officials, and most of the time, it's best that you don't. When the game is about to begin, the officials are focused on doing their job, so support them in that focus and let them know you wish them well, rather than potentially distracting them.

The officials will likely return your positivity, and you'll all be prepared to perform your best.

## How to handle adverse situations

At this point, you are now fully aware of what you can do to create a positive pre-game experience and a solid foundation for a positive in-game experience. I've taken you from the moment officials arrive to the moments before the game begins.

Now you might be wondering, "This all sounds great, and I'm going to try to do these things, but what happens when something goes wrong?"

I'm glad that you're asking that question, because the way in which we handle adverse situations and potential conflict says a lot about our commitment to having the best possible experience. As a coach, you know that the game doesn't always go according your game plan, and you have to be able to deal with any adverse events that arise that threaten the success of your plan. You know how to handle these situations without thinking about them very much, but now we need to think about what might happen to our game plan with the officials.

So let's talk about what to do when things don't exactly go as planned in the pre-game phase.

## The same rule still applies

The rule that I laid out at the beginning of this chapter with regard to your pre-game interactions with officials still applies in adverse situations—be cordial at least, friendly at best, but always positive.

Remembering and following this rule will serve you well in any situation that comes up that might stand in the way of creating a positive pre-game experience. It will also help you work with officials to overcome the situation in a way that maintains your ability to work together.

Let's look at two simple examples of adverse situations that might come up and how you can successfully handle them. Once you understand these examples, you'll be able to handle anything that might happen.

## Example 1: Addressing the unexpected

Sometimes, things are going to happen that you couldn't or didn't expect, and they will threaten the quality of your pre-game experience. Your team is going to arrive late to the game, you'll have to deal with a crisis, you won't be able to find the key to the officials' facilities, you'll have to address a crisis and your lineup isn't ready on time. These things, or similar things, *will* happen. What matters is how you deal with those unexpected things so that they don't derail your pre-game experience.

I've got another simple framework for how to handle these situations, and it involves three steps. If you like acronyms, you can call this one the "Triple-A Plan."

1. Acknowledge.

2. Apologize
3. Accept and move on.

The first thing that you need to do is acknowledge what has happened. Then apologize for it (even if it isn't your fault). Then accept the consequences and move on.

Let's take the first situation, where your team is late for the game. Maybe you got lost, or you got bad directions, or there was unexpected traffic—whatever. It doesn't really matter what caused the situation; what matters is how you handle the situation.

As soon as you can, apologize to the game management and the officials (it's even better if you can contact them ahead of time, before you even get there; if you do that, still follow-up when you arrive). Something simple like, "Oh man, I'm really sorry we were late. Really sorry. We'll get dressed and be ready as soon as possible." You don't have to offer big explanations or excuses, just acknowledge the problem and apologize for it.

Everyone who has been involved in athletics understands that things like this are going to happen. They don't want to be jerks about it. What they do want is for the responsible party to act responsibly about it. That's you.

A lot of times, you'll find that this disarms people's potential frustration and makes them much more likely to respond with compassion. I've been to games where a team has been late, and even if it is their fault, they handled it in the way that I've mentioned, and the home team agreed to push the start time back so that they would have time to get ready without being totally stressed out.

The same goes for some situation that might affect the officials, like that missing key I mentioned. Acknowledge the situation and apologize. Something like, "I'm really sorry, we can't seem to find the key. I'm going to get on this and we'll get you sorted out. Again, I really apologize." Just saying something that simple can put the minds of the officials at ease and signals to them that you care about the pre-game experience.

Sometimes, there are consequences attached to unexpected events. Let's take the example of being unable to have the lineups ready on time. If this is a rule in your sport, there is likely a penalty attached. Once you know you've broken the rule, acknowledge it to the officials, apologize for it, and accept the consequences. Chances are, if you acknowledge it and apologize for it, officials will do what they can to mitigate the potential penalty. Remember, they're following Samford's Law, so they don't want to begin a game with a penalty. Your acknowledgment and simple apology will make them more likely to apply the law.

## Example 2: Addressing problems that are your responsibility

There are going to be times when a situation arises that might be adverse for you, but is still your responsibility to handle. Once again, how you address that situation with the officials has an impact on the pre-game experience and the tone you are setting for the rest of the game.

Bear with me as I share a personal example, because I think it highlights this situation very well.

Some years ago, NFHS changed the basketball regulations with regard to how the coaching box was to be measured, marked and administered. The measurements were relative only to the existing court measurements, and nothing else.

If you know anything about high school basketball gyms, you know that each one is unique, and that means that the location of bench areas is sometimes different from gym to gym. The new rule didn't care about the potential differences in benches, however; it dictated that the head coach was only permitted to stand inside the box, and if their particular chair was outside of the box, they were not permitted to stand. They could either move the chairs, or sit in a different chair that was within the box.

Because of this rule change, we made sure that coaches and administrators knew about the new coaching box measurements, along with how they were to be implemented and enforced, during the preseason scrimmages. (We always use scrimmages to try to iron out wrinkles in new rule enforcement.)

During the first week of the season, I was the crew chief for a game. We walked out onto the floor and noticed almost immediately that the home team didn't have the coaching box properly marked for either team, and they had chairs outside of both boxes. It also just so happened that the coaching staffs were sitting in those chairs during warm-ups.

While we were observing warm-ups, as a crew, we discussed what we were going to do. We knew we had to tell each coach about the situation and inform them of the potential consequences, along with the potential ways they could fix it. As the crew chief, it was my responsibility to tell them.

After walking to the scorer's table to approve the score book, I walked down to the head coach of the home team to have the conversation about the benches. I started with the home team because it was their gym, so they needed to know how to address this for future games. I could immediately tell that he saw me coming and didn't want to talk.

"Hey coach, I hope you're doing good tonight." I started.

"Hey," he replied, without standing and hardly looking up. Not a good start.

"Look, I'm going to need your help with the coaching boxes. I noticed that you don't have the boxes properly marked. So you're going to have to get someone to put a tape lines down, or you're not going to be able to stand during the game."

At this point, the coach let out a heavy sigh and shook his head. "Okay, I'll get someone to do that."

He was clearly perturbed. It may or may not have had something to do with the coaching box situation, but whatever it was, he was clearly in a less-than-positive mood. Now, I was just trying to resolve this situation without it escalating into some sort of confrontation.

"The other thing is the chairs. You can have chairs outside of the box, but if you sit in those chairs, you can't stand. If you want to stand, you can either move those chairs into the box, or leave them and sit in different chairs. It's up to you, but if you sit outside the box, you can't stand."

Now I had the coach's full attention. He stood up from his chair. He was still not happy. "I'll put the tape lines down, but I'm not moving any chairs."

Now this had gone from a simple notification of a potential rules violation to a potential confrontation. That was the last thing I wanted. Samford's Law was foremost in my mind. I just needed to resolve the situation before it escalated further.

"Okay, coach. That's fine. You can leave the chairs where they are, but you just can't stand if you sit in those chairs outside the box. Good luck tonight."

With that, I turned and headed down the sideline to the visiting coach.

He saw me coming, stood up, and reached out his hand to shake mine. I shook his hand. "Hey coach, I hope you're doing good tonight."

"Yeah, we're doing okay, thanks," he said. We were already off to a better start.

"Look, I'm going to need your help with the bench over here. I've already told the home coach that the coaching boxes need to be properly marked, and he's going to get someone to put some tape down, so that's taken care of. But if you sit in these chairs that you're currently sitting in, you won't be able to stand, because the chairs are outside of the box. So you can either move these chairs, or you can sit in different chairs that are inside the box. It's up to you."

At this point, the coach does exactly what I've been advocating to you and says, "Oh, I'm sorry, we didn't realize that. We'll probably just sit in different seats."

The coach acknowledged and apologized for something that he didn't even need to apologize for, and our interaction was over. Simple and positive.

I went back across the floor to my crew, who both had a pretty good idea of how the two interactions had gone down. We all agreed this game was getting off to a tense start.

## Why it matters

You might be reading my example and wondering why it matters. Did it affect the the calls I made in the game? To answer the last question first—no. It didn't change the calls that my crew had to make in the game. Like I said before, officials are trained to brush that kind of stuff aside when the game starts. But what it did do was force our crew out of the positive environment that we strive to create before every game. Instead of lightening the mood, it made things more tense. It heightened our awareness of things that we shouldn't have to worry about before a game even starts. It put everyone on

43

edge, even if only for a minute.

If both coaches had reacted like the visiting coach, things might have gone differently. The pre-game environment would have been slightly more positive.

In the end, the game was intense and the reaction of the coaches to the pre-game situation was indicative of how they would handle themselves in the game. I wish it had been different. It *could* have been different.

These little interactions, and how we handle them, matter.

## Knowing we've screwed up and learning from it

I think that the home coach in this situation screwed up. He could have handled our interaction better. I have no idea what put him on edge, but he let it affect his interaction with me, and ultimately with our crew. Maybe he learned from that—I might never know. I officiated many games for him after that, and we never had another interaction anything like that one ever again, so maybe he did; or maybe that was just a bad day.

I'm also aware that I screwed up in that situation. I broke Samford's Law in a rush to keep it. I broke it by not talking to both coaches at the same time. I put sh*t in the game by not setting all of us up for the best possible outcome in that situation. We all need to hold ourselves accountable in these situations and honestly evaluate how we can make them better in future games.

As I said, I never had another adverse situation with that coach again, so I like to think that we both learned something that night, and we're both better for it.

## The wrap-up

Now you have some tactics and strategies for the pre-game phase of your game plan for interacting with officials. Let's briefly review what we've covered:

- In all of your interactions, be cordial at least, friendly at best, but always positive.

- Make sure you're handling the things you're responsible for handling.
- When something unexpected comes up, utilize the Triple-A Plan (acknowledge, apologize, accept and move on)
- Remember that small positive gestures can have a major impact, so think of the small ways you can create a positive pre-game experience.

The pre-game experience lays the foundation for a positive in-game experience, so resist the temptation to brush off the pre-game and focus solely on your in-game plan. If you spend just a little time and effort on making your pre-game experience a positive one, you can turn your tactics into habits that will become fundamentals in your interactions with officials. You'll get to a point where you won't have to think about doing these things, you'll just do them at every single game. Developing that consistently positive pre-game experience will pay dividends in your coaching career.

In the next chapter, I'm going to cover the phase of your game plan that probably motivated you to pick this book up in the first place—the in-game experience. Just as with the pre-game phase, I'll share with you strategies and tactics that can make your interactions with officials more positive, and we'll go over ways to handle the inevitable conflicts that arise between you and the officials. Implementing these strategies and tactics will help you get the results that you want from the officials on your game—and improve the overall in-game experience for everyone involved.

# 5

# In-Game

*"We talked to the referees before the game; there's always new situations to adjust, for the refs and for us as well. Even on the ice, it's good for players to talk and interact with the referee."*
*—Peter Bondra*

Now it's time to talk about what happens during your in-game interactions with officials. This is the most prominent phase of your game plan for interacting with officials. It is the one that you have probably already thought about the most, and it's probably the one that you are most eager to address. Let's direct that enthusiasm at creating a win-win.

I'm probably going to say some things that you didn't expect to hear, or maybe I'm going to say some things that you've heard before, but in a different way. Either way, I'm going to ask you to be as open as possible to the things I'm going to cover in this chapter. At least give them some consideration.

I know you've been doing that already, and I appreciate it. In many ways, the things that you've learned so far are building up to the in-game phase of your game plan, so we need to hold all of those things together to create the winning game plan that you want.

If we can do that, then not only will your in-game interactions with officials improve, but you'll have a better experience, your players will have a better experience, and you'll be a better coach.

Let's jump in...

## Perfection is the goal

Remember that your overall goal in this game plan for your interactions with officials is to win, and you win by getting the most possible consistency out of the officials on your game. Every phase of the plan has its own unique goal that serves that overall goal. Just as the pre-game phase of the plan had a unique goal of laying a strong foundation for positive interactions with officials, the in-game phase has a unique goal.

The goal of the in-game phase of your game plan is simple to state, but harder to achieve: perfection. Yes, the goal of the in-game phase of your plan is to have the perfect game.

Now, the "perfect game" has a very specific meaning in this context. Here's how we define the "perfect game" for the purpose of interactions between coaches and officials:

**The perfect game is when coaches and officials never have to interact.**

Did you just hear the needle scratch loudly across the record? Good.

I want to get your attention with this. I want to get your attention and I want you to be open to considering the goal and definition of the perfect game (remember what I said a few paragraphs ago?).

## How can this be perfection?

You're probably asking yourself something along the line of, "how can a game where I never interact with the officials be considered a perfect game?"

The reason why a game where you never interact with the officials is a perfect game is because, first of all, it means that you never had a *reason* to interact with them. That means that nothing happened in the game that required your involvement with the officials. That means—no major problems.

But it means something else, too. It means something even more important. Not interacting with the officials means that you were able to spend one hundred percent of your time and attention where you should have been spending it: coaching.

From the officials' perspective, if they never have to interact with the coaches, then both of those things are also true—there weren't any major problems, and they were able to spend one hundred percent of their time and attention on officiating.

That sounds a lot like perfection to me.

## Interaction is distraction

Ultimately, you're at the game to coach your team, and the officials are at the game to officiate the game. To do them well, both of these jobs require significant concentration. When coaches and officials interact, they are reducing their concentration on their respective jobs to have those interactions. You don't need that distraction. Officials don't need that distraction. Distraction reduces consistency. Everyone does a better job when everyone is one hundred percent focused on doing their particular job. Interaction is a distraction, no matter how small.

## Is perfection even possible?

I'm willing to admit that a game in which you never have to interact with the officials sounds impossible—but it *is* possible. It is possible because many interactions between coaches and officials are voluntary. To be sure, there are situations that will arise in games that require you to interact with the officials, or require the officials to interact with you; but if none of those situations arise in a game, it is certainly possible that you could go an entire game without ever interacting with the officials.

The perfect game is the ultimate goal, just like winning is *your* ultimate goal. I'm guessing that you didn't begin your coaching career assuming that it was possible to achieve the goal of winning in every single game you coach, but

IN-GAME

the fact that you won't win every game doesn't stop you from giving your best effort toward achieving that goal in every game.

You should approach your game plan for interacting with officials the same way you approach your general game plan: do everything you can to achieve the ultimate goal. You might achieve the goal; you might not. But if you do everything you can in pursuit of the goal, you will know that you did your best, and you'll know where you might be able to improve, or how to handle situations differently in the next game, to get you closer to your goal.

Overall, continually pursuing the goal of having that perfect game where you never interact with officials will improve your experience in games, the exact same way that continually pursuing the goal of winning improves the performance of your team.

Now that we have an ultimate goal in mind for the in-game phase of our game plan for interacting with officials, let's start to take a look at what can be done to reach that goal.

# The killer tactic

There is one very simple thing you can do that will serve the goal of having the perfect game, while also feeding the motivation of the officials and allowing you to coach to the best of your ability. This is the killer tactic for interacting with officials in a game that, if you can master it, will do more for you, and for the officials, than anything else you can possibly imagine. This tactic is like hitting a grand slam, scoring a touchdown on a kickoff after getting a safety, getting an and-one on a made three-pointer, and scoring on a penalty, all rolled into one.

**LEAVE THE OFFICIALS ALONE.**

I know what you might be thinking right now: "WHAT?! Daniel, come on, man. You told us this book was about how to interact better with officials, and now you're telling us to leave them alone? That's crazy!"

That's exactly what I expect you to say. But like I said at the beginning of this chapter, stick with me.

Remember what I said about the definition of a perfect game? When you don't interact with the officials, it means two things: there were no major issues, and both the officials and the coaches were able to concentrate one hundred percent on doing their jobs to the best of their abilities.

When you leave the officials alone, they're able to concentrate on doing their jobs, and you're able to concentrate on coaching. That is better for everyone.

And I'm going to let you in on a little secret: the officials don't want to interact with you, if they don't have to. It's not that officials don't like coaches; it's that officials want to be able to do their jobs without distraction, because their jobs require a lot of concentration. For that reason, every official is trained not to seek out interactions with coaches unless those interactions are necessary. Officials don't want to create distraction for themselves, and they don't want to create distraction for you, either.

When you leave the officials alone, I can almost guarantee that they will leave you alone. And I can almost guarantee that if you can get really good at leaving the officials alone, every official who works one of your games will want to be there, and they will want to come back, because they know you are providing them with the best possible environment to allow them to do their jobs to the best of their abilities.

Leaving the officials alone means that you will get more motivated officials, which means those will be better officials, which means that those will be more consistent officials.

When you master the tactic of leaving the officials alone, you'll be serving the goal of the officials, but just as importantly, you'll be serving your own goals, and you'll be able to devote more time and attention during games to what really matters to you—coaching.

Leave the officials alone. It's better for them, and it's way better for you.

# Implementing the killer tactic

Now that I've given you the killer tactic, you're going to have to implement it. I don't expect that you'll be able to just go out in your next game and never interact with the officials. You don't expect your players to immediately pick up and implement every tactic you give them. You have them practice it over and over. You give them drills to do. You give them complimentary tactics they can use.

I'm going to give you some complementary tactics that you can use while you're working your way to leaving the officials alone, and some tactics that you can use when you've done everything you can but still find yourself having to interact with the officials. Using these tactics will still help support your goal of working toward the perfect game, without interfering with your officials' motivation.

## Use a diplomat

The first, and most strenuous, objection I hear to the killer tactic is that you need to interact with the officials because you need to communicate to them certain things you might see in a game, or things that you might need from them. That's a fair objection. Notice, though, that the killer tactic is for *you* to leave the officials alone. The ultimate goal is for *you* to avoid interacting with the officials during the game. I never said you couldn't *communicate* with the officials. That would be silly.

So how are you going to communicate with the officials if you can't interact with them? Easy: use a diplomat.

What's a diplomat? Most of the time, when people refer to a diplomat, they are referring to the person who speaks with a foreign country on behalf of their country's leader. Historically, the diplomats came about when kings and queens had courts. Each court had members from foreign countries who were called diplomats. It was the job of the diplomat to speak to the ruler of the court on behalf of their ruler, and to take official messages back and forth between the two rulers. The diplomat was a trusted person who allowed the

51

two rulers of two countries to communicate in an official way without having to interact in person.

Are you beginning to see how a diplomat might work in the context of the in-game relationship between you and the officials?

I want you to think back to what I said in the pre-game phase of the game plan about picking a good captain. I said that, ideally, you should trust your captain to be able to interact with officials. When that isn't possible, you should at least know which player(s) you *do* trust to interact with officials, just in case that *needs* to happen.

If it sounds like that person would make a pretty good diplomat, you're exactly right. Ideally, it would be a captain, but if not, that's okay. Just know which players you can trust as diplomats to enable you to communicate with officials without having to interact with them.

The reason that using a diplomat is so effective relates to what I said earlier about officials' desire to be preventive officials. As I said, they don't want to interact with you if they don't have to, but they still want to address issues, so they'll do that through the actual players in the game as much as they possibly can. Having a diplomat complements the desire of the officials perfectly: you can get your message across to the officials, and the officials can interact with the players, instead of with you, which they would rather do anyway. Everybody wins.

Having a diplomat also does at least two things for you, as a coach. First, it increases your communication with players. More communication with your players is good for you because it shows your players that you are paying attention to them, and it allows you opportunities to reinforce your coaching.

The second thing having a diplomat does is provide a buffer between your emotions and the officials, which can prevent interactions that result in trouble. You get emotional in games. Officials *expect* you to be emotional—they don't expect you to be a robot. But when there are negative interactions between coaches and officials, it is often because the emotion of the situation got in the way of effective communication. Having a diplomat can give you a buffer that keeps the emotion from spilling into an interaction, and it keeps the communication clear and effective.

Here are two of the most prominent reasons to use a diplomat to communicate with the officials.

## Example 1: Getting better consistency

Let's say that the game has been going on for a while, and it looks like your team is being called for a particular violation, but the other team isn't. Maybe you've even noticed the officials have missed some clear instances against the other team. It's really starting to bother you. That's understandable.

If you bring this up to the officials yourself, it might not go so well. You are frustrated by the inconsistency and your frustration might come across in a way that leads to a negative interaction. This is the perfect opportunity to use your diplomat. Call them over and say, "Hey, can you ask the officials to watch the violations?" Then, all that player has to do is go to the official, let him know what your team is experiencing, and ask him to look out for it.

I can guarantee that the officials will listen to what the player has to say. You get to communicate your message, the player and the officials have a positive interaction, and you've left the officials alone. Everybody wins.

## Example 2: Getting an explanation

By far, the most frequent event that leads to negative interactions between coaches and officials is the disputed call that results in a penalty/foul/violation. It doesn't always have to be that way, though. Many times, what you want as a coach is an explanation of what the official saw and was calling. But again, the emotion of the situation can make that difficult to communicate. This is a great opportunity to use your diplomat. Here's a real-life example from one of my games that hammered home the value of the diplomat strategy for me:

Toward the end of a close game—a super-intense game with a big crowd—there was a block/charge play at the basket. I called a block, resulting in a foul for the home team and free throws for the visitor. Every point was precious in this situation. It was obvious to me that the home coach didn't agree with me—he was pretty upset. I expected that, and I knew that if we had an interaction about the call, it probably wouldn't be a positive one. I could tell that he was trying to get my attention to talk about it, but I also knew that little good would come from us interacting in that moment. Emotion was too high. I needed him to focus on coaching and finishing out this game on a positive note. But he also needed an explanation of my call. At this point, he employed his diplomat. He got the attention of the player who was standing closest to me during the free throws and said, "Ask him what he saw!"

The player got close to me and said, "Sir, what happened on that play?" I gave my explanation to the player; he ran over to coach and quickly relayed it to him. It was clear from his reaction that the coach disagreed with me, and that was perfectly fine, but he accepted the explanation, and we moved on to finish out the game on a positive note.

Had the coach persisted in seeking to interact with me directly, the interaction probably wouldn't have been positive, but he needed to communicate. Specifically, he wanted an explanation. By using his diplomat, he was able to get the explanation he wanted (and deserved) without having a potentially negative interaction. He was able to go back to coaching, and I was able to go back to officiating. Everybody won.

The block/charge is a situation in basketball games that can lead to confrontation, but it can be diffused with a diplomat. I'm sure that you can think of similar situations in your sport where you could use a diplomat to get the explanation that you want while avoiding the potentially negative interaction with the officials.

## Use diplomats to your advantage

Using the diplomat is a great way to work toward implementing the killer tactic of leaving the officials alone. Think about the situations that come up in your games where you feel the need to interact with the officials, and then consider whether you could have a diplomat handle that communication on your behalf. If you can, you'll be able to maintain communication with the officials while also reducing your interaction with them. You'll be well on your way to implementing the killer tactic and keeping the officials motivated.

Your diplomat will be incredibly valuable, so choose that player carefully. Make sure that your diplomat is a player who you can trust to positively interact with the officials. The last thing you want to do is send a diplomat to the officials who ends up getting themselves—or worse, both of you—kicked out of court.

The best way to prevent that is to have in mind some tactics for communicating with officials that you can teach your diplomat, and that you can use when you do have to interact with officials.

## How to interact, when you must

As much as we want to hit our goal of the perfect game, it is inevitable that interaction between you and the officials will happen. And even if you do manage to reach the goal of a perfect game, your diplomat is going to need to know some tactics for interacting with officials. So let's go over some easy tactics that you (or your diplomat) can use when you *do* have to interact with officials.

First, recall what I said about the strategy for pre-game interactions in the last chapter. It still applies to interactions in-game: be cordial at least, friendly at best, but always positive.

This strategy is especially important for in-game interactions because, as we've already touched on, in-game interactions have a greater chance of being contentious and potentially negative. There are times when you will have interactions that will fall into the "least" category, and you'll have to just be cordial. There are times when you will have interactions that will fall into the "best" category, and you'll be able to be friendly. No matter which category a particular interaction falls into, though, you always have an opportunity to conduct that interaction in a way that has a net positive impact on the in-game experience.

## Tactic 1: Keep things brief, and expect brevity in return

Think back to our goal of having a game with zero interactions between you and the officials. If we're going to run into a situation where we can't reach that goal because you *need* to interact with the officials, we should at least try to get as close as possible to the goal. That means that we need to restrict to our interaction to being as brief as possible.

Why do we want to keep things brief? Think about it this way: If you can't reach your goal of winning a game, you don't want to get blown out, right? Of course not. If you can't win, you want to get as close to winning as possible. You want to give yourself a chance to win. Similarly, keeping your interactions with officials brief gets you as close to your goal as possible.

You should also expect officials to implement the same tactic when they need to interact with you. They also want to be as brief as possible. Brevity reduces the chance for conflict to occur, and it forces officials to be direct. Officials also want to be brief because they don't want to waste anyone's time. They want to get back to officiating, and they want you to get back to coaching. In-game interactions aren't the place to get into long discussions. Say what you need to say, then get back to coaching.

Being brief doesn't mean being terse or rude. Remember to always keep the strategy above in mind. You can be brief and cordial. You can be brief and friendly. You can be brief and positive.

## Tactic 2: Ask a question

This tactic applies mostly to cases when you are the one initiating the interaction. When you want or need to interact with the officials, one of the most effective ways to set a good tone for the interaction is to ask a question. This is a tactic that good officials will use just as often as you use it. In fact, if you think about a lot of your interactions with officials, you'll probably recognize it. If you go back and look at every example I've shared in this book, you'll see the question tactic being used.

Let's look at an example. In this example, we're going to combine asking a question with being brief for optimal effectiveness (you'll find you can usually use these two tactics together).

The official makes a call you don't agree with. You want to voice your disagreement because you want to show your players that you're working for them. That's fine. Here's how you do it:

You can say to the official, "Hey, what did you see on that play?"

This is both brief, and a question. The official knows that you likely disagree with the call, because if you agreed, you wouldn't ask; but when you ask a question, you're engaging the official in a way that they can respond without conflict. There is a saying that I learned about interacting with coaches early in my officiating career as a guide for interacting with coaches: "Statements can be ignored, questions deserve a response."

When you ask an official a question, they ought toshould respond (if they can). In this case, the official is going to tell you what they saw. They're going to be brief about it. They'll probably say something like, "Coach, your kid [insert explanation here], so I had to call it."

At this point, the best option is to stick with being brief and cordial and to say something like, "Okay, thanks for the explanation." If you feel an overwhelming need to voice your disagreement, then the best way to do it is stay brief and cordial and say, "Okay, I didn't see it that way, but thanks for the explanation." You've been brief, cordial, and positive (with the "thanks"). Well done.

At this point, you've said what you needed to say, and the official has heard you and addressed it. You can both go back to doing what you are there to do.

## Tactic 3: Seek help

Remember what I said in the beginning about officials being helpers at heart? Well, this tactic uses that motivation of officials in a way that can improve your interactions and get you what you want in many situations. This is also a tactic officials use in their interactions with coaches and players, and if you think about your interactions, and you look back at my examples, you'll see it. Here's how it works...

You want the officials to do something. Don't tell them what to do, though; instead, enlist their help.

This is another tactic that can be combined with what we've already learned to create maximum effectiveness for everyone. That means you can be brief, ask a question, and seek help all at the same time.

Let's say that your players are being persistently fouled, and it appears that either the officials are missing it, or they aren't calling it. Your players are starting to get frustrated. You need this to be called. That's fine. Here's how you do it:

"Hey, can you help my players out with the fouling? They're getting frustrated and I don't want it to escalate. I appreciate it."

The official is now aware that you think they are missing (or failing to call) something. They also know that you have a valid reason for asking them to look at it more closely (your players are getting frustrated). You've asked them for help with the situation.

More often than not, you'll find that officials appreciate this kind of interaction. They appreciate it because officials are helpers at heart, and they are also team-oriented. This kind of interaction shows that you want their help, and that you can work together on the issue.

If you do something like this, it is possible that the official is going to respond with, "Okay, coach, I'll look for it." They also might respond with a question like, "What do you mean, coach?" or "Which play are you talking about, coach?"

If the official does ask a question, remember to stick to being cordial and brief. The official is asking because they genuinely aren't aware of the issue and they genuinely want to address it. You can respond with something like, "They've got hands all over my number thirty-two. If you could just watch for it, thanks."

The official will probably end it with, "If that happened, I missed it. I'll look out for it, coach." Or just, "Okay, coach, I'll look for it."

You've been brief. You've asked a question. You've enlisted the officials to help. Your concern got addressed, and everyone has been brief and cordial. Good job.

## Use the Big Three to your advantage

Now you know the three most important tactics you can use for your in-game interactions with officials. By using one of these in an interaction, you'll do well. Use two of them together, and you'll have success. If you can work hard on using all three of these tactics together, you'll find that your interactions with officials will be more positive, and you'll start getting the consistency you've been looking for.

You're not going to change the officials' minds by using any of these tactics—don't think that all of the calls are going start going your way all of a sudden. What you *will* be doing, however, is influencing the mindsets of the officials. You'll be setting up a relationship built on cooperation and mutual respect. You'll be setting up the kind of relationship that will deliver the maximum consistency from the officials and the maximum performance from you. Everybody will win.

# The wrap-up

We've covered a lot of important ground in this chapter. Let's go back over the major points again:

- The goal of every coach and every official during every game should be the same: the perfect game. The perfect game is when coaches and officials never have to interact. This means everyone gets to do their job with one hundred percent concentration.
- The killer tactic for creating an environment that officials want to work in is simple: Leave the officials alone. Do your job well, and let them do theirs.
- The best way to use the killer tactic is to find and use a diplomat on your team. This allows you to leave the officials alone while still being able to communicate with them.
- When you must interact with the officials, try to use at least one, but preferably all three of these tactics: Be brief. Ask a question. Seek help.

These are the highlights, but definitely re-read this chapter as much as you need to so that you can really understand the details and implement the things we've talked about here. You've been keeping an open mind so far, and I really appreciate that. It's a credit to your commitment and professionalism. Keep your mind open and try to think of as many ways as possible that you can practice and implement these tactics in your in-game interactions with officials. The more you can commit to them, the better your in-game experiences will be with the officials, and—who knows—you might even have a perfect game along the way!

Now that we've covered the pre-game and in-game phases of your game plan for interacting with officials, it's time to move on to the post-game. I'm going to show you how you can use the time immediately after a game (or the time in between games) to create an environment that will benefit you and your team and promote the consistency you want.

# 6

# Post-Game

*"The game is never over. No matter what the scoreboard reads or what the referee says, it doesn't end when you come off the court."*
**—Pat Summitt**

The buzzer has sounded, the official's whistle has blown, the last out has been made, the clock is reading all zeros...in other words, the game is over. Now what?

While the game might be over, that doesn't mean that your work is done, or that your game plan is finished. The post-game phase involves all of that time between the moment the game ends and the moment the pre-game phase for the next game begins.

The post-game phase of the game plan is critical for two reasons:

First, post-game is the time when you can continue the positive impact you've made during the pre-game and in-game phases—and extend it all the way until the next pre-game. The post-game phase is a bridge that connects one game to the next, thereby establishing a continuous and consistent commitment to winning with officials and creating a positive environment.

Second, the post-game phase is the time when you can have a significant positive impact on your coaching reputation with the people who wield the most influence over the officials. We're going to cover how you can manage your coaching reputation in another chapter, but there is a lot you can do during the post-game to set you up for a shining one.

If you want to win with the officials and set yourself up for a positive reputation with the people who matter the most, then you need to use your time in the post-game phase of the plan as wisely as possible. There are three ways you can wisely spend your time during the post-game phase, and if it helps, you can remember them by using the acronym, "REP."

1. Time for **R**einforcement.
2. Time for **E**valuation.
3. Time for **P**reparation.

There are aspects of the post-game phase that fit into each of these times, and there are some that will fall under all three, but by spending your time wisely in the post-game phase, you can maximize the positive impact of your post-game activities. Let's walk through the post-game phase chronologically, starting with the end of a game...

## Minimal interaction but opportunity for reinforcement

Discussing *time* in the post-game phase is a bit ironic, because it is the phase in which you will spend the least amount of time actually interacting with game officials. But even though you will have little, or maybe even zero, interaction with game officials in this phase, there are still a lot of ways to reinforce what you've done pre-game and in-game, along with making a positive impact toward the success of your game plan in future games.

Once the game is over, in most sports, the officials are going to try to exit the field of play as quickly as possible, and (hopefully) with zero interaction with players or coaches. In some sports, the officials might linger and shake hands with the players or coaches. It just depends on the sport.

This means that the interaction between coaches and officials is limited as much as possible once a game has ended. This makes sense, when you think about it: After a game ends, emotions are often at their peak, and no one wants a negative interaction between the officials and the coaches or players as a result of high emotions. That's not good for anyone, and it can have an impact on the game in question (or future games, depending on how penalties are administered in the sport).

The reason I'm even talking about this non-existent, or at least minimal, interaction is because it has the potential to either reinforce or destroy your positive interactions up until this point. This is the first moment in the post-game phase when you can use your time to reinforce the positive environment you created in the pre-game and the positive interactions you've (hopefully) had during the in-game.

Reinforcing this positivity is easy. If you are in one of the sports where officials try to leave without interaction, let them do so. They're not going to be offended or upset, because they're not expecting or trying to interact with you. Just let them go. If something odd happens and you do happen to make eye contact with them or something, remember and use what you've learned so far: be cordial or friendly, but positive. A simple smile and acknowledgment is great. Saying, "Thanks, drive safe," works, too. But don't seek interaction. Just let the officials leave. That's all they want.

If you're in one of the sports where there is minimal interaction with the officials immediately following the game, then again, use that time wisely by using it for reinforcement. Be cordial at least, friendly if you can, but positive. Shake hands, thank them, wish them well, and head to the locker room. That's it.

If you think that the time immediately after the game is a good time for you to air grievances with the officials or talk about plays, you are wrong. Very, very wrong. Just let the officials leave.

This doesn't mean that you can't air grievances, or talk about plays, but it does mean that you need to do those things at the appropriate times, in the appropriate ways, and there is a time during the post-game phase that you can use wisely for that, if you so choose, but it definitely is not the time immediately after a game has ended.

You might be thinking, "Well, if I don't do it right after the game, I'm going to forget it later."

Maybe. But if you forget about it later, then it clearly wasn't important enough to remember. If it wasn't important enough to remember, then you definitely didn't need to bring it up right after the game was over.

Remember that there is a time and place for everything, and in the post-game phase, you want to use your time wisely for the right things. Use the time immediately after the game has ended to reinforce your commitment to a positive relationship with officials by being as brief, friendly, and positive as possible.

## Locker room talk?

After you've left the field/court with your team, the next phase of the post-game time is usually spent in the locker room. This is another time that you can use wisely by applying the strategies and tactics you've already learned to address your team and reinforce your commitment to positive interactions with officials.

As with the in-game phase, when you were trying to reduce your interactions with officials to as few as possible, you want to reduce your words *about* officials in the locker room as much as possible. Preferably, to zero.

There really isn't anything you can say about the officials to your players that will improve the relationship among you, your players, and the officials. During my days as an athlete, nothing I ever heard my coaches say about officials in the post-game locker room was positive or helpful. Thankfully, hearing them say such things was rare.

There is another reason that you don't want to talk about the officials to the players, and it is a more practical one: it creates an excuse. I know that, as a coach, you don't like excuses from your players, so don't allow them to use the officials as one.

I know that there will be times when officials will make mistakes that will have an impact on the game. I know this because I've experienced the mistakes as a player, and I've made such mistakes as an official. It sucks. It hurts. But ultimately, you can't control the officials, and neither can your players. And trust me on this: the officials are aware of their mistakes, which I'll address in more detail shortly. For now, you just need to know that talking to your players about the officials in the immediate post-game time usually doesn't improve anything. Not talking about the officials during that time is the best way you can make use of that time, because it allows you to focus on the players, who, most of the time, are the ones who matter.

## Interviews

After your time in the locker room, there are some of you who will be asked to do interviews or maybe attend a post-game press conference. If this is you, this is another time that you can use wisely to reinforce your commitment to positive interactions with officials while also having a positive impact on your reputation.

All you have to do is follow the strategies and tactics you've already learned and applied. This is another time that can most wisely be spent by not talking about the officials at all. And again, if you must—if you are asked about the officials—apply what you have already learned: be cordial at least, friendly at best, but always positive.

The main reason to use your interview time this way is because this is a time when everyone can hear. Up until this point, your interactions have been limited to officials, your players, and your coaches. Once you are talking to members of the press, anyone and everyone can hear what you are saying. That means that the people who have the most influence over the officials, and over your work, can listen. The last thing you want to do is give them something to listen to about the officials. Many leagues, districts, conferences, etc. have specific rules against addressing the officials in the press. If so, follow these rules. If they don't have rules, make one for yourself and don't talk about the officials. If you do that, you'll have nothing to worry about.

When you do this, you'll be avoiding potential problems and headaches that can come from such comments. Every moment you have to spend dealing with those problems and headaches is a moment you can't spend doing what really matters to you—coaching.

Like I said, there is a time for everything, and there are going to be times when you are going to want, and maybe even need, to talk about the officials, but a post-game interview is not one of those times.

With that being said, let's take a look at times and ways that you can talk about the officials. If you stick to these times and ways of talking about the officials, you'll be able to address what you want to address in a way that has a positive impact on your relationship with the officials and on your reputation as a coach.

## Get it off your chest

Sports are emotional. The games can be intense. You care deeply about doing the best job you can do, about helping your players, and about winning. Those are all good things. Sometimes, the officials will do something that gets in the way of those things and makes them more difficult, and that will make you upset. I get it. I know it will happen.

If you're committed to having better relationships with officials, getting more consistency from officials, and getting better officials on your games, then you need to understand how those mistakes get handled from the officiating side, and you need to understand the best ways for you to deal with those mistakes.

First, let's talk about what you can do. As I've already mentioned, using the time immediately after the game to address your grievances with officials is very unwise. So what *should* you do?

If you absolutely must—I mean MUST—say something to someone in the immediate aftermath of a game, I can understand. Just don't do it around the players. Don't do it around the press. Don't do it around the parents. Do it in private. I know that it can help to vent your frustration in order to keep from bottling it up or exploding. So, if you need to vent, do it in an environment that won't make things worse for you or your team. Maybe that means you spend a few minutes alone. Maybe that means you talk to your coaching staff in private. Maybe that means you write it down and then throw it away or delete it. How you do it is entirely up to you, but if you need to vent in the time immediately following a game, make sure that you do it in a way and in an environment that won't have a negative impact on you or your relationships with the officials.

## Time for evaluation

Now that you've gotten through the immediate post-game period, there is some time for evaluation. You might have a few moments for this evaluation on your trip home or back to the school, or maybe in the days between games. Whenever you have some down time, spend a bit of it wisely by evaluating how well you executed your game plan for the officials.

You don't have to do an extensive break down, as you would with the game film. All you have to do is spend a few minutes and ask yourself these three questions:

1. Did I do everything I wanted to do for the officials?
2. Did anything happen that had a negative impact on the game plan?
3. Is there anything I could do differently to address (1) and (2)?

First, just think back and make sure that you did the things that you wanted to do. Were the officials treated as you wanted during the pre-game? Did you have the right captain/diplomat? Did you limit your interactions as much as you wanted to?

Next, consider any interactions that weren't ideal, or might have had a negative impact on the game plan. It was probably something during the in-game phase, but maybe not. If anything really sticks out in your mind, you'll probably want to evaluate it.

Finally, honestly evaluate anything that came to mind with the first two questions, and consider how you might be able to do things differently in the future to get the result that you want. That might mean changing how you do things, or it might mean adding or taking away from things that you do. Just be sure to give it some honest consideration.

This process shouldn't really take you more than a few minutes, and implementing any changes should only take a few more, but you'll definitely feel the impact of using some of your post-game time wisely to evaluate how things went with your game plan.

The more frequently you go through this process, the less time it will take, because you'll find yourself getting better and better at executing the game plan.

## Prepare wisely

The time in-between games can also be used wisely to prepare for the next game. Much like the evaluation phase, the preparation phase doesn't have to take a lot of time, and it will take even less time, the more often you do it. Also like the evaluation phase, the few moments you do take to prepare can have a big impact on the success of your game plan in the next game.

Part of your preparation will be the result of your evaluation. If there was anything that came up in your evaluation that you need to address for the next game, prepare to do so. Talk to anyone you need to talk to, or keep in mind anything you need to keep in mind to improve the execution of your game plan.

### Should you practice?

When you are preparing your team for the next game, a key part of that preparation is obviously practice time. That's when you get to make changes to what you do as a team, implement new things, and reinforce the things you want.

I suggest thinking of ways that you might be able include practicing how your athletes are going to interact with the officials. You don't have to do any specific drills or anything, but think about the ways that you might be able to simulate what it is like to interact with officials. Maybe that means having someone act as an official during your game simulations. Encourage your athletes to use the same simple strategies and tactics you've learned. Doing so will serve to make your team more prepared, and it will serve to reinforce the environment that you want to create.

## Know who's coming

Sometimes, you might even know in advance who the officials are that are working on your game. If that is the case, consider how you have interacted in the past, and if there is anything you can do to make things even better in the next game. Hopefully you've had a great relationship with the particular officials and you're looking forward to seeing them. If your relationship might have been strained in the past, consider this an opportunity to execute your game plan better and build a strong foundation for the future relationship. Every game is an opportunity to win with the officials, no matter who they are.

## The wrap-up

The post-game phase provides you with time and opportunity to improve the execution of your game plan for the officials. If you wisely use the time between the end of one game and the beginning of the next one, you have an opportunity to do three things that will help your "REP:"

1. **R**einforce your overall commitment to a positive relationship with the officials.
2. **E**valuate your game plan and how you might be able to improve it.
3. **P**repare for the next game in a way that sets you up for success.

Even with few or no interactions between you and the officials during the post-game phase, there are plenty of ways you can reinforce, evaluate, and prepare. The good thing is that none of the tactics in the post-game phase take a lot of time, but all of them can have a big impact. And the more frequently you put these tactics to work, the less often you will have to think about them because they will become ingrained into your game plan for officials.

In the next chapter, we're going to talk about what you can do when things go wrong. Let's be honest: officials are going to make mistakes. We all know this. What you can do is handle those mistakes in ways that work with your game plan and help promote a positive relationship with the officials. Let's take a look at just what you can do...

# 7

# When Officials Screw Up

*"Some of the best preparation I had for coming to Congress is being a football referee. Because you've got to make a decision, and no matter what you do, someone's unhappy with you."*
—Suzan DelBene

I've hinted at this, but now it's time to talk a bit more about something that is inevitable when dealing with officials: screw ups.

This might come as a shock to you, but officials screw up.

Now that you're done laughing, let me assure you that officials know they are going to screw up, too. They know that no matter how much preparation they do, the game in which they make every single call correctly is an impossibility. Honestly, that iwas one of the things that I liked most about officiating—I knew that no matter how well I did, there was always room to do better. The opportunity for improvement is endless.

But for you, as a coach, that isn't much consolation when an official has made a mistake that has an impact on the game. Officials know that, too.

In this chapter, I want to share some ways that you can handle mistakes from officials, or even grievances with them, in ways that will support your goal of building a positive relationship. Conflict is inevitable, because it is part of the relationship between coaches and officials, but the inevitable conflicts can be handled in ways that are good for everyone involved and that form a basis for more positive interactions.

I'm going to illustrate the positive ways you can handle conflicts with officials using examples from my own officiating career. Before we get into the tactics and the examples, though, I think it will be helpful for you to understand just how the evaluating of officials is handled. Many people have the mistaken belief that officials aren't really accountable to anyone and never suffer any consequences for their mistakes. The reality is quite different: officials are very aware of the mistakes that they make, and there are plenty of people around them who are ready to hold them accountable and help them learn.

## The three types of mistakes

I'm going to speak in the broadest possible terms for the purpose of this book because what I'm saying should apply across just about every sport. If we were talking about a specific sport, we could get more detailed, but for right now, I don't think we need to do that.

Broadly speaking, there are three categories of mistakes that officials can make:

1. Errors in mechanics.
2. Errors in judgment.
3. Errors in rules application.

In the world of officiating, category three is considered the worst of the three possibilities. That's because the officials are the people who are primarily responsible for knowing every rule and how it is to be applied. There is no acceptable reason for messing up a rule. That doesn't mean that it never happens; it just means that it is a serious error when it does happen, regardless of the impact on the game.

Just as officials are expected to know the rules, they are also expected to know their mechanics. Mechanics are the physical actions that officials take in order to effectively officiate. This covers everything from how an official blows the whistle, to their positioning, to the use of their signals. There is a lot more flexibility in evaluating mechanics because personality has an effect, and there are sometimes multiple mechanics that are effective in any given situation. That being said, errors in mechanics often lead to errors in rules application and errors in judgment.

Errors in judgment are the most common errors and the ones that everyone loves to talk about during and after the game. These are the errors that are to be expected, because no official has perfect judgment, and there are a lot of factors that can impact judgment on any given play.

Officials are always being evaluated for their mechanics, judgment, and rules application. In fact, they are often being evaluated on more than one level.

Let's take a look at how the evaluation of officials often works...

## On being evaluated

No matter what sport it is, the officials are always being evaluated. Usually, there are multiple layers of evaluation. The potential layers are as follows:

1. At the very least, every official is self-evaluating.
2. Every official is evaluating the other officials working on their game as part of the crew.
3. There might be an observer at the game who is evaluating all of the officials in person.
4. There might be someone who watches video footage of games at a later time to evaluate the officials.
5. The supervisor or commissioner is ultimately responsible for evaluating the officials.

That's five potential layers of evaluation for every official, in every game. And even in rec-league or AAU games, at least that first level of self-evaluation exists. As a result, officials are very aware when they have made mistakes, and there is usually someone there to evaluate and help them learn from mistakes.

At the higher levels of officiating (NCAA and professional), officials are often evaluated for every single play in a game. That means that someone is evaluating every situation in which an official did make a call, or could have made a call, and then the accuracy of that call or non-call is evaluated for judgment and rules application. The official then gets a score, from from zero to one hundred, that reflects their overall accuracy. Zero would mean the official did nothing correct, and one hundred would mean that the official made no errors. This score affects the official's schedule, whether or not they get to work in postseason tournaments, and whether or not they remain on staff.

In the high school and rec-league/AAU levels, there usually isn't this level of detail in the evaluation of officials in each game, but there is still a lot of important evaluation that goes on in every league and with every association of officials.

While coaches are being evaluated on the basis of wins and losses, officials are being evaluated on the basis of accuracy and consistency, and these evaluations have consequences.

## When mistakes are serious

Now that you have a better understanding of how officials think about mistakes, and how they are evaluated for making them, let's talk about the kinds of potential mistakes that you care the most about.

First, we're going to talk about the kind of potential mistakes that are serious enough that you, as a coach, want to make sure someone knows about. In my experience, those kinds of situations fall into three categories:

1. Something that leads to an email from the supervisor within a few days of the game.
2. Something that leads to a phone call from the supervisor on the way home from a game.
3. Something that leads to a phone call or visit from the supervisor in the

locker room after the game.

I want to tell you that I have been involved in all of these situations. Some of them were the result of mistakes I made, or that my crew made, and some of them weren't mistakes, but still needed to be evaluated to determine if my crew or I did the right thing.

My point in telling you this is twofold. First, I want you to understand that officials are aware of their mistakes, and they are aware of the situations that occur that could be evaluated. They are also aware of the potential consequences of mistakes. Second, I want you to understand that there are ways that you, as a coach, can address these situations or mistakes in a way that improves your relationship with the officials.

I'm going to use two examples from my own officiating career to illustrate how these situations can be handled in ways that improve your relationship with officials, and in ways that don't improve your relationship, and might even damage it. My hope is that you'll chose to handle these situations in ways that can reinforce your commitment to a positive relationship with officials because doing that will not only be appreciated by the officials, but will serve to increase your reputation as a coach.

## My first college game

I had one of these situations in the very first regular-season NCAA basketball game I ever officiated. Because it was my first game, I was on a crew with two of the most senior and experienced officials in the conference, and my conference supervisor was at the game to observe.

It was the first home game of the season for the home team. There was a lot of excitement and the game was very close. All in all, it was a great first-game experience for me. In fact, the game was coming down to the final possession. The game was tied, and the home team had the ball with less than ten seconds on the clock. Obviously, they were going to run a play to get the last shot.

They successfully ran a play, and passed the ball to a wide-open player in the middle of the lane. He went to the basket and scored as time expired. The crowd went wild.

Except...

There I was, blowing my whistle and emphatically waving off the basket for a traveling violation on the player who scored what everyone thought was the winning basket. The mood of the crowd instantly changed.

As a result, the game went into overtime. During the time waiting for the overtime to begin, the home coach was understandably upset, but my parter did what he should have and protected me. He talked to the coach and the coach seemed to understand. What could have been a very negative outcome in that moment ended up being as positive as could have been hoped, given the circumstances.

The home team eventually lost the game. As you can imagine, our crew left the floor as quickly as possible at the final buzzer.

When we got to the locker room, we were there about ten seconds before a man started beating on the door, screaming obscenities—obviously less than thrilled about my traveling violation call. He was there for a little while before we heard his voice fade away. That was when my supervisor walked into the locker room.

First, let me say that I completely understand that guy's reaction. Like I said, games get emotional—but that's not the way to handle it. This, by the way, is why I said that you don't want to be the person that allows their emotions to take over and lead to a reaction that can damage your relationship with the officials: that guy got carried away, and then he literally got taken away by security. Don't be that guy.

When my supervisor walked in, he started with, "Geez, who was that guy? He's crazy. Security is taking him away." Without missing a beat, he knew exactly what everyone in that room was thinking and he addressed it. He looked me dead in the eye and said, "The last play in regulation. What did you see?"

I wish I could say that I was supremely confident in what I had called, but given the situation and reaction, I was a bit nervous. Nevertheless, I explained what I saw and why I called the violation. I then held my breath.

"You were exactly right."

I exhaled.

"Not everyone would have the courage to make that call. Good job. If the coach or the AD has anything to say, I'll talk to them, but good job."

## A tale of two reactions

I'm telling you this story to contrast two reactions: those of the coach and of the man who beat on our locker room door.

The coach in that situation could have hit the ceiling. In fact, I'm sure there were more than a few people who probably expected him to have that kind of reaction. But he didn't. Sure, he was emotional and upset; that's perfectly understandable. But he didn't scream at me and there was no finger-pointing at me. He talked to my partner, my partner talked to him (to this day, I have no idea what they said to each other), and we moved on to the overtime. Even after losing the game, he didn't try to stop me from going off the floor (I had to run past his bench). He didn't say anything to me. He didn't need to. I had a pretty good idea what he was thinking, but he didn't say anything. That mattered.

I did another game for him a few weeks later. I'm sure he remembered me, but he didn't say anything about that previous game. We both moved on and went about our jobs. I did a few games for him during his time in the conference, and we actually ended up having a good working relationship. A lot of that was due to how he handled that particular situation, and how he handled the aftermath.

On the other hand, the guy who spent time banging on our locker room door and screaming obscenities at us had to be removed from the venue by security. On our way out of the venue, the school officialgame personnel who was in charge of us told us not to worry, that he probably wouldn't be allowed back for a few games, at least. I have no clue whether or not that was true, but it did show that the school was committed to maintaining a positive environment for, and relationship with, game officials.

I also don't know if the AD or coach ever followed-up with my supervisor. If they did, they did it the right way, through the right channels, and they got the answers that they were looking for, even if they weren't the answers they wanted. They showed their commitment to maintaining a positive relationship with the officials.

And that's the point—everyone was committed to doing the best that they could do and maintaining a positive environment and relationship. That night, even in the wake of a controversy and an undesirable scoreboard, everybody won.

## The night I put sh*t in the game

That was an example of a time that there was controversy, but after evaluation, it turned out I had made the right call. I'd be lying if I told you that things always work out that way—that's definitely not always the case. Here's a personal example of a night that I violated Samford's Law and it blew up my game. This is a long example, but I think there are a lot of lessons to be learned, so stick with me.

It was the very first game of the high school boys' basketball season, and I was working at a school I had worked at dozens of times before. (It is no coincidence that my previous example and this example both occurred in the first game of a season. Officials are a lot like coaches and players in that they are working out the kinks at the beginning of the season, too, and they usually get better as the season goes on.)

The visiting team was from out of the area, so I had never seen them or their coach before. That's not unusual at the beginning of a season, but it always adds another variable to the game, because it is an unknown.

I was the crew chief on the game, and one of my two partners on the game was someone whom I had never worked with before. This was his first varsity boys' basketball game. Officials always consider it an honor whenever we can work with someone on their first game of any sort; so this was exciting for the crew.

The game progressed as normal. No issues. It wasn't a particularly close or intense game, but it was a little sloppy, which is to be expected in the first game of the season for both teams. We had absolutely no issues with either coach, and we barely even interacted. Things were going as well as could be expected. Until...

A player on the home team scored a basket on a contested layup and fell to the floor. There was no foul on the play, but when he got up, he and an opponent got in each other's faces and began taunting. I was the official closest to the play, so I called a double technical foul (one technical foul on each player for unsportsmanlike conduct).

After we got everyone separated, we came together as a crew to make sure we all knew what was going on and how to administer the penalties (no free throws, and we would resume play from the point of interruption—meaning the visiting team would have the ball). I reported the fouls to the scorekeeper, and my partners watched the players. As is often the case when something like this happens, the coaches each called their teams over to their benches.

Upon bringing the players out from their benches to resume play, the player from the visiting team who received the technical foul threatened to beat up his opponent after the game. At this point, I called a second technical foul on that player, which resulted in his ejection.

Now, we had a lot of things going on. The player being ejected was upset, the visiting coach was upset, and now we had to switch from a throw-in to free throws and giving the ball back to the home team. So far, though, there wasn't anything going wrong, just a lot going on.

The visiting coach wanted, and was owed, an explanation for the ejection. I went to him and explained what had happened, at which point he admonished his player for what he had done. The coach wasn't happy about it, but that didn't surprise me. Our interaction was intense, but as brief as possible. I started to head back to my position for the free throws that we needed to shoot. (As a general rule, the officiating crew is trying to get play resumed as quickly as possible—getting everyone to return their focus to the game usually helps calm things down.)

This is the moment at which I made my first mistake and put sh*t in the game, although it wouldn't become apparent right away. I didn't use the proper mechanics.

What I was *supposed* to do, after talking to the coach, was make sure that a substitute was entered into the game for the ejected player. In my desire to be brief with the coach and get the game restarted as soon as possible, I failed to make sure the sub was provided. That was my responsibility. I failed.

On the way back to my position for the free throws, one of my partners approached me and said that he had pulled his calf. In-game injuries to officials are rare, but they do happen. I asked him if he could finish the game (we were less than three minutes from the end). He said he thought he could.

At this point, I made my second mistake—also a mechanics error. I chose to switch positions with my partner. I knew if we switched, we could keep him in the "center" position for as long as possible, thus reducing the amount of running he would need to do on his injured calf. My motive for changing the mechanic was a good one, but it had the effect of relocating me to the opposite side of the court from the team benches and the coaches. This reduced my ability to communicate with and monitor the benches in what was obviously a tense situation. As the crew chief, I shouldn't have done that. In any other situation, changing that mechanic would have been fine, but in this particular situation, it would end up making things worse—as you'll soon see.

We went through both free throws for the technical foul, and I was the official in charge of the throw-in to resume play, which takes place at half-court, opposite the benches.

We still didn't have a sub at this point. Remember, I screwed up by not making sure the sub was in the game at the right time. This is where the visiting coach did something that I definitely don't recommend and that didn't exactly contribute to improving the situation, even though I understand what he was doing. He knew that the sub was supposed to be in the game, but he withheld the sub, because he still wanted to talk to me about the ejection.

So allow me to set the scene at this particular moment. I was across the floor from the coach, he was yelling at me to get my attention, and we didn't have the right number of players on the floor. I saw him calling for me, but at this point, we'd had our discussion. Further discussion wouldn't have resulted in anything positive, so I was just trying to get play started.

This was when I made my third mistake, yet another mechanics error: I failed to count the players before I put the ball into play. This is a fundamental mechanic that every official knows; it's called "sweeping the floor." Ideally, before you ever put the ball in play, but definitely after some kind of interruption in play (like three technical fouls, two free-throws, and an injury to an official), you quickly scan the floor and count to make sure you have ten players, and then make eye contact with your other officials so you know everyone is ready to restart. I didn't do that. As a result, I put the ball in play with five players from the home team, but only four from the visiting team.

It was the home team's possession, so we were on the opposite end of the floor from the visiting coach. At this point, he was HOT. He was jumping up and down and screaming. The home team scored a quick basket, and we began heading to his end of the floor. As we were doing that, I looked across the floor at him, because he was yelling and gesturing at me, and I realized he was saying he didn't have enough players. I quickly scanned the floor, realized he was right, and blew the whistle to stop play.

Now we were at the moment when all the sh*t that I'd put in the game through my errors in mechanics really hit the fan. The coach was furious, partially because he didn't agree with my technical foul to begin with, and now because we'd played an entire possession without his full complement of players. He was yelling at me and coming out on the floor.

I immediately went to him and apologized for the error. He was yelling about how could we start the game without all five players; I told him, "You're right, coach. That's my fault. I should not have done that." I'm going to talk about this in just a bit, but it's worth noting that there are circumstances under which an official will tell you that they made a mistake. In a little bit, I'll show you how you can recognize those circumstances and use them to strengthen your relationship with the officials. Unfortunately, on this night, I think our relationship was a bit too far gone.

This was when he admitted he had been holding the sub back in an effort to get me to come over to him to talk about the ejection. I told him that now was not the time to talk about that, and that we needed to get his sub and restart the game.

And then we were at a stalemate. The coach was so mad that he was refusing to put his sub in the game; I couldn't restart the game without his sub. The last thing I wanted in this situation was to escalate it further, so I used the final tactic that I had to hopefully put an end to things: I told the coach that I was going to start the clock for the substitute to enter the game, and I told the the coach that he could yell at me as much as he wanted for those fifteen seconds, but at the end of them, the sub had to enter the game, and we had to move on. I instructed the timer to start the substitution clock. I stood next to the coach while he berated me. To be honest, I didn't mind that. I deserved it, to a degree, and I hoped that allowing him to blow off steam would put an end to the situation.

The buzzer sounded, and the sub came onto the floor. I said, "Okay, coach, now we're done," and I walked across the floor for the throw in. He followed me, yelling that we weren't done. I didn't want to give the coach a technical foul. I knew that wasn't going to help the situation, but then he actually said to me, "I'm not going anywhere unless you give me a tech." I obliged.

We again shot free throws, put the ball back in play, this time with the right number of players on the floor, and finished the game. You can believe that we left the floor as quickly as possible. It wasn't a great way to start the season.

Back in our officials' locker room, we began to break down what happened as a crew, and now that's what I want to do with you...

## The breakdown and the lessons

A lot of people are tempted to evaluate a situation like this and focus on the calling of the technical fouls as the spark that caused the game to burn down. But the reality is that those calls had to be made. They were unavoidable, as they were all related to the sportsmanship and safety of the players. Each one was earned by the players. What *could* have gone differently was the aftermath.

Looking back over the entire incident, there were a few things I did wrong, all of which made the conflict worse:

1. I should have followed proper mechanics and made sure the sub entered the game immediately after talking with the coach. I allowed my desire to explain things to the coach to interfere with my responsibility to ensure

that the sub came into the game.

2. I should not have switched positions with my injured partner. I allowed my desire to protect the health of my partner to interfere with my responsibility to ensure the free throws were properly administered and to hear the coach, who was withholding the sub in an effort to speak with me.

3. I should have swept the floor. I allowed my desire to get the game going again to interfere with such an important mechanic.

Those were the lessons that stuck with me, from an officiating perspective. I'm bringing them up because I want you to understand that I was aware of each of these mistakes almost immediately after I made them. And by the time I stopped the game to get the sub in the game and talked with the coach a second time, I had a full picture of just how my mistakes had put a truckload of sh*t in the game.

## The aftermath

Remember when I told you about the three kinds of serious situations that officiants can find themselves in? Well, this one fell into categories one and three. In fact, I called my supervisor from the locker room, because I wanted him to know what happened and about the ejection before he received a call from the state high school league. My supervisor agreed with the calls I made and my assessment of the mistakes I made. A few days later, he called me and asked for an official report on what led to the ejection, because it was required for the high school league (that was only the second time, and so far the last time, that I have ever ejected a player or coach from a game). I wrote my report, and that was the end of the situation. The high school league found nothing wrong with the fouls or the ejection, and the player received his penalty for it.

## Lessons for coaches

Just as there were lessons that I learned from this incident that have stuck with me ever since that night, I think there are some instructive things to be learned from what the coach did in this situation.

First, coaches need to understand that officials do not want to call violations that lead to serious penalties. Almost always, they are called out of necessity and as a last resort. They obviously elicit a lot of emotion, and officials understand this, too. So try as hard as you can not to let the emotion of the situation cloud your judgment and do something you wouldn't otherwise do.

Next, don't try to use the rules of the game to manipulate officials. In this case, the coach was withholding the substitute because he knew I would have to come to him to get the sub, and then he could talk to me more. Now, it didn't work, because I screwed up the substitution, but even if it *had* worked, it would not have led to the outcome that the coach wanted. Using the rules as leverage to get the officials to do something you want demonstrates that you don't want to work with the officials, you want to control them. That's a terrible message to send. There are always better ways to get the reaction that you want, and sometimes, you don't really need any reaction from the officials. The coach in question actually did this a second time when he refused to put the sub into the game and asked me to call a technical foul on him. Did he get the reaction he wanted? Sure. But it did nothing to help the game, and it cost his team more points. That's a terrible tradeoff if your goal is to win with the officials and create a positive environment.

## Getting what you want, the right way

If this wasn't the best way for the coach to get what he wanted, that raises begs the question—

*How can a coach get his concerns about the mistakes of the officials addressed in a way that helps him win with officials and reinforces a positive environment?*

84

I'm glad you asked...

## Addressing the mistakes officials make

Let's go back to the types of mistakes that officials make and discuss how you might be able to address them in the right way.

First, let's talk about the in-game mistakes.

The first thing that to understand about addressing the in-game mistakes that officials make is that you need to be extremely selective. If you start trying to point out everything you think the officials are missing, you're in trouble. That will have the opposite effect that you are seeking. Instead, if you feel you must address a possible mistake, make it only one or two per game. Keep in mind that, if a mistake was made, the official is likely already aware of it; when you do choose to address it, try to use the same tactics that you've already learned about interacting with officials. That means:

1. Be brief.
2. Ask a question.
3. Enlist help.

## EXAMPLE:

A play occurs that results in what you believe to be a missed call. It is perfectly acceptable to question the official about it in a way along the lines of, "Are you sure about that one?" The official is going to answer your question; accept their answer and move on. An even better way to address the official is to say something like, "What did you see there that made you call that?" This will, again, engage the official in a way that prompts them to respond. An official should be able to answer both of these questions. Once the official does respond, it is possible that you won't agree with them. If you don't, you can simply say, "Okay, I didn't see it that way, I thought <insert what you saw here>." The official will acknowledge that, and you've been able to get your point across in a way that reinforces your commitment to working with the officials (rather than arguing with them or trying to control them) and maintains the positive environment.

You'll know this is the case, because the official will likely respond with something like, "Okay, coach, that's fair" and you'll know you're really making progress if the official says, "Okay, coach, if that's how it happened, then I missed it."

During these in-game interactions about potential mistakes, you need to understand that you're not going to get the officials to change a call, even if they missed it (unless it is something that is allowed to be reversed, by rule). But if you handle these in-game interactions the right way, you'll build trust and a positive relationship with the officials that will help you win by motivating the officials to work with and for you, likely giving you more consistent officiating.

You'll know that you are reaching that goal when you address a possible mistake by an official and they say something like, "Yeah, I missed that one, coach. I'll work harder to get them right." An assurance like this shows that you have reached the pinnacle of trust from officials. That is because, as I said earlier, officials will admit mistakes to coaches, but they'll only do so with the coaches that they know they can trust to respect them, and they're only going to do it once in a game, if they do it at all.

If you think I'm pulling your chain, I want you to consider a statistic. In 2017, the National Association of Sports Officials (NASO) conducted a survey of more than 17,000 sports officials. They asked a lot of different questions, one of which was:

"Have you ever admitted a mistake to a coach or players during a contest?"

You might be surprised to learn that 13,864 officials said that YES, they had admitted a mistake to a coach or players during a contest. That's over eighty percent of the officials surveyed.

If you've never had an official admit their mistake to you, it might be because they don't have the level of trust in your relationship that they would like to have. If you can put into practice the tactics that I've shared with you for addressing the mistakes of officials, I think you'll find that it will gain you respect and increase the trust officials have in your relationship.

## Addressing the serious issues

Let's talk about how you can effectively address the potential mistakes that occur and lead to serious situations. These are the types of things that you think need to be addressed by your league, or by administrators, or by someone above the in-game officials. These are situations that can only be addressed after the game has ended.

First, as we saw in the previous chapter, if these situations are that serious, you never want to address them directly with the game officials after the game. There is no good that can come from that confrontation. None. Leave it alone.

But that doesn't mean you need to be quiet about it. If the situation does need to be addressed, just make sure that you address it to the proper people through the proper channels. The people and channels are going to vary by sport, league, and level of play, but there is always some way for coaches to address these issues.

Usually, this is going to involve an email or a phone call to someone who can then relay the message to whoever is in charge of the officials, or to the officials themselves. When you're going through this process, always make sure that you are doing so with the highest level of professionalism and that you let the people responsible do what they are supposed to do. I know that it can be hard to put these situations in the hands of others, but these processes exist for a reason.

If you handle your grievances in the way that they are supposed to be handled, you'll earn the respect of the officials because you're showing them you are as committed to maintaining a positive relationship as they are. You'll also earn the respect of your administrators and league officials, which helps increase your reputation on and off the field/court.

## The wrap-up

We've covered a lot of important ground in this chapter, and I hope it has given you a better understanding of how you can address the mistakes of the officials in a way that serves your goal of winning with them and demonstrates your commitment to building and maintaining positive relationships. If you can put the things you've learned in this chapter to work for you, you'll find that it will not only yield results in your games, but also increase your reputation with the officials and your administrators and league officials.

Let's take a quick look at some of the highlights of what we've covered in this chapter:

- Officials are always being evaluated in their games, by themselves, or by others, or both.
- Mistakes by officials can be divided into errors in mechanics, errors in judgment, and errors in application. There are the normal in-game mistakes that can be made, and also the more serious mistakes that are usually addressed after a game.
- How you handle the mistakes officials make can serve either to reinforce or damage your game plan and commitment to creating and maintaining positive relationships with the officials.
- For in-game mistakes, you should address them very selectively, but always by being brief, asking a question, and enlisting help.
- For serious mistakes that need to be addressed after a game, never address them directly with the officials and always make use of the proper channels and proper people for addressing such situations.

Officials are going to make mistakes. They are going to make them on your games. It is inevitable. How you choose to address those mistakes will go a long way to either reinforcing or damaging your game plan and your relationship with the officials. When you choose to do the things that reinforce your relationship with the officials, you'll find that you get the immediate benefit of improving the environment for the officials and likely their performance. You'll also achieve the long-term benefit of a more positive reputation with the people who have the most influence over officials and over your job—administrators, league officials, and officiating supervisors/assignors.

It's that long-term benefit of a good reputation that we're going to talk about in the next chapter. If you want to go all the way in winning with officials and experience a true transformation in your relationship with officials and the officials on your games, this next chapter is for you...

# 8

# Respect and Reputation

*"You don't demand respect, you earn it."*
—*Steve Seidler*

I want you to think about someone you've encountered in your coaching career who has an unassailable reputation. It could be a coach you worked or played for, an administrator, or anyone else you've come in contact with. I want you to think of the person who has the best reputation you can imagine, the person that you would drop everything for if they needed something, or do anything they asked—because you know you can trust them and they would only ask you to do the right things.

Do you have that person in mind? Good.

I want you to keep them in mind during this chapter, because we're going to be learning about the importance of reputation for you with regard to the officials and administrators you work with and under. I want you give you some tips to help you build a reputation with the officials and the administrators that is equal to the reputation of the person that you're thinking about right now. I want to help you do this because if you can do it successfully, it will be better for you, the officials, the players, and the game.

In this chapter, I'm going to tell you what qualities officials and administrators look for in a coach. Remember what we said a few chapters ago—you want officials who want to work for you.

You also want administrators who want to work *with* you. When you're able to achieve this kind of reputation, you'll notice that your relationships with the officials and the quality of the officials on your games will both improve. This improvement will lead to a reduction in the frustration you might currently feel about the officials.

This chapter is going to include some hard realities about how you end up with certain officials on your games, how you sometimes end up with the officials you have on your games, but these are realities that you need to understand and account for, if you're going to have the kinds of relationships that I think you want to have.

If you've ever felt disrespected by the way officials interact with you, or by the selection of the officials to work your games, the odds are that you aren't being disrespected—it's just that the officials probably find you difficult to work with. But if you put to work the things that you've already learned in this book, you'll be well on your way to motivating officials to want to work with you. That means you'll be earning their respect and building your reputation.

Building a positive reputation is something that does require work, and it might even require you to change some of the things you've been doing, but if you've gotten this far in the book, that means that you've already shown a commitment to doing what is necessary to have a positive impact. Now, it's time to follow all the way through...

## How did I get these officials?

I want to begin with an overview of how officials get assigned to games. I'm going to speak in broad terms here, because there are differences in the different levels of officiating, and I'll talk about some of the reasons for those differences.

The reason that I want to bring this to your attention is so that you'll have a better understanding of how this aspect of the world of officiating works—because it has a direct effect on your games. I'm sure you've had some officials on a game who made you think, "How in the world did this person get assigned to my game? There had to have been someone else they could send." Once you understand how officials do get assigned to games, it will help you prepare your game plan and prepare yourself for in-game interactions. This understanding will also reinforce the importance of having the best possible reputation with the officials and the administrators, which is what this chapter is ultimately about.

## Who picks the officials?

No matter what league you are in or at which level you coach, someone is in charge of the officials for your games. Generally speaking, that person is called the assignor. That's because they assign officials to the games. That person might also have other titles, because the people who administer officials often have to wear multiple hats, but it's the hat of assignor that we are going to focus on for right now.

As the assignor, they receive the schedule of games for which officials are being requested. This comes from the league director, or the athletic directors of schools, or even the individual team coaches. This is one of those points at which there can be some differences between leagues and levels.

As the assignor, they are responsible for knowing the officials on their staff or in their association. They're responsible for knowing the officials well enough that they know their general personalities, along with their talents, skills, and experience levels. Every official is different, and the good assignors know these differences in their officials.

Once the assignor has games to assign, they have to look over who is available among their officials and choose officials to work on the games. This is often a rather complex process, because the assignor can't just pick whoever they want for every game. I guarantee you that every assignor has a few officials that they would prefer to pick for every game if they could (because officials have to work on their reputations, too), but of course that's not realistic.

If we're only talking about one single game, the assignor first has to see which officials are available on that day/time, and then factor in many other variables, such as the location of the game relative to where the official is traveling from, other games the official has recently worked, the personalities of the coaches, the personalities of the officials, and any history that might preclude an official from working for a particular coach or at a particular school, just to name a few of the variables.

Now, when you multiply this out over multiple games per night, for multiple weeks in a season, things can get very complicated for the assignor, very quickly. It's not an easy job, but it's a critical one, as you can imagine.

There are also factors that are beyond the control of the assignor when it comes to scheduling. The biggest one is the number of available officials. I worked in a high school basketball officiating association that often had every single official in the association working on a Tuesday or a Friday night (those were the busiest nights). That meant that if someone got injured, or sick, or wasn't available for some reason, the assignor's job became much more difficult.

The reality of a lack of available officials is something that a lot of sports are having to deal with at every level of officiating (with the exception of professional sports—*everyone* wants to work at that level).

## Why this matters

I want you to understand a little bit of what assignors have to deal with so that you can hopefully see how it affects your own games. To go back to the question from before— "How in the world did this person get assigned to my game?"—there are going to be times when the answer to that question is, "This was the best official available."

I also want you to understand that the assignor is an official, too. Sometimes, the assignor is a currently-working official, but at the very least, the assignor is a very experienced former official. That means that the assignor is governed by the same philosophies as the officials they assign. Most importantly for you, that means that the assignors are trying to be preventive officials, too, and they also don't want to have any problems in any of the games they assign.

From their perspective, that means they want to match the best officials they can to the games that they have to assign. As I mentioned just a bit ago, there are a lot of factors at play in trying to match the officials to the games, but I can guarantee you that the assignor wants a problem-free game just as much as the officials do, and now, just as much as you do.

This means that an assignor is always going to do their best not to put you or the officials in a situation that could lead to unnecessary conflict or a negative outcome. For example, in the high school association that I worked for, it was not uncommon to have to work multiple games for a team within ten days. The assignor always did his best to avoid this situation, but there were times it was unavoidable. As a result, if I had a situation where I had to give a technical foul to a coach, and I was scheduled to see them again soon, I would usually be reassigned to a different game. It wasn't that I had done anything wrong, nor was it any kind of punishment; it was just preventive officiating on the part of the assignor. Similarly, the assignor would try not to assign officials to work for a particular school too many times in a month. This was again, preventive. It prevented coaches from getting tired of seeing the same officials, and vice-versa. People like variety.

The key points that I want you to take away from this introduction to assigning games is that assignors have a tough job that they take seriously. They are officials just like the game officials, which means that they want to do their best, they want to be preventive, and they don't want any problems.

Just like with your game plan for the game officials, if you can contribute to meeting the goals of the assignor, you'll find that it increases your reputation, it improves your relationships, and it makes the officials want to work for you.

## Keeping the bosses happy

Now that we've looked at the people who are responsible for the officials (assignors/supervisors), let's look at the people who are responsible for you—administrators.

No matter what kind of coaching you do, there is someone to whom you are ultimately responsible—there might even be more than one person. If you are a coach in a school, those people are probably the principal, the athletic director, and whoever runs your high school league. If you're a coach in a recreational/amateur league, you are responsible to whoever runs that league. Now, I know there are some structures that are outliers, where teams can be largely independent, but even in that situation you need games, which means you are often responsible to tournament directors, at least.

The point I'm trying to make here is that you have bosses. Your reputation with those bosses matters. The better your reputation with them, and the better your relationship with them, the better your coaching life will be. If you can keep the bosses happy, it will go a long way to keeping you happy.

If you think again about the person I told you to have in mind at the beginning of this chapter, I'm sure you'll find that they had a stellar reputation and relationship with their bosses, whoever those people might be. Those strong relationships were partially the result of their good reputation, which was a direct result of how they conducted themselves on and off the field.

Every school administrator, league director, or tournament director I've ever met had something in common with the officials: just like the officials, administrators don't want problems. They don't want problems because problems complicate their jobs and lives, making things more difficult than they need to be.

That's where having and following your game plan for the officials and using some of the tactics I'm about to reinforce can have a major positive impact on your reputation: they are all designed to prevent problems from happening—and solve problems when they do happen.

If you can be the kind of coach who works to prevent problems, and solve problems when they do happen, you will gain the respect of the officials and the administrators, your reputation will improve, and your coaching career will benefit in more ways than you might have expected.

## Follow the game plan all the way through

If you remember how I introduced you to the game plan for officials, it was about understanding the officials and the ways in which their goals and your goals can be reached together. Now, I hope you have some understanding of how following that game plan all the way through, from pre-game, during in-game, and through post-game, will also meet the goals of the administrators who are responsible for the officials, and for you.

If you can commit to working the game plan all the way through, at all times, in as many ways as you possibly can, you will establish a reputation as the kind of coach that officials want to work for, and that administrators want to work with. You will gain the respect of the people that you need to improve your experience and your relationship with game officials.

You've come this far in learning about the game plan. If you can actually put it all together, and follow it all the way through, it will take your career as a coach to new heights and improve the experience for yourself, the officials, and your athletes. You'll not only see better officials on your game, you'll be a better coach.

# 9

# Ready for Success

*"Success is peace of mind which is a direct result of self-satisfaction in knowing you did your best to become the best you are capable of becoming."*
—*John Wooden*

Right now, you are in a pre-game situation. I have no idea what stage of your season you are at—maybe you are reading this during the season, maybe it is the off-season, or maybe it's pre-season and games are about to begin. No matter what time of the year it is, though, you now have the game plan you need to bring the about the success that you said you wanted with the officials.

You picked up this book because you want to get better officials on your games. That's an understandable desire. I hope that, through understanding officials better, you now understand what it means to have better officials. Here are some things you now know that can help you:

- You know that officials are motivated by being helpers, they're motivated to do their best, and they're motivated by their love for the game. Those are things you have in common with the officials on your games.
- You know that, above all, officials don't want to have problems in their games. For their part, officials achieve this goal by using preventive officiating and following Samford's Law.

- You know that you want to have officials on your game who want to be on your game. The way to get those officials motivated to be on your game is to prepare for their success and yours.
- You know that having a game plan for the officials will prepare you for success with the officials just like having a game plan for your team prepares you to win the game.

I've shown you that creating a game plan for the officials and doing simple things will show the officials that you are committed to having a positive relationship and helping them meet their goals for each game. Here are some ways your game plan can help you:

- You can use the pre-game phase of the game plan to create a positive environment that will lay a strong foundation for your interactions with officials during the game.
- You know that the goal of every game should be not to have to interact with the officials; but you also know *how* to interact with the officials in ways that will reinforce your commitment to a positive relationship with them.
- You have a plan for wisely using all of the time in the post-game phase, from the end of a game to the beginning of the next one, so that you can maximize the impact of that time to reinforce your commitment to a positive relationship with officials that benefits all of the participants in your games.

When you review everything that you've learned in this book—all of the philosophy, strategy, and tactics—you should be able to grasp how putting it all to work for you will gain you the respect of the officials and administrators, increase your reputation, lead you to better experiences with the officials, and ultimately make you a better coach.

Now you just have to put everything you've learned into action. You've got the plan, now you need to execute it. You're at the critical point that you've brought your players to time and time again: it's time to take all the learning and planning and put action behind it so you can win the game.

That is my most sincere wish for you: that you win with this game plan. It is my sincere wish because I know that if you are able to win with this game plan, the officials will also be winning, and it will lead to a better experience for you, them, and the athletes. We all love the game, and I truly believe that following this game plan will benefit the games we all love.

# 10

# We need Officials. You can Help.

*"We do need maybe younger or more experienced judges but where you can get them I don't know. It's like in football, who would want to be a football referee? You'd just get criticism all the time."*
—*Callum Smith*

There is a nationwide shortage of sports officials. This is not my opinion; this is a well-documented fact. In high school associations across the country, directors are feeling the crunch of not having enough officials to work the scheduled games. This shortage is already affecting schedules in many areas of the country, where games are having to be rescheduled, and Friday Night Lights are having to become Wednesday or Thursday Night Lights due to a lack of officials. If it isn't happening in your sport, or in your area, count yourself lucky, because if the current trend continues, massive changes to the way we schedule high school sports are coming. All of it is due to the inability to recruit and retain sports officials.

The National Association of Sports Officials (NASO) conducts research surveys of its members on various topics. They survey more than 17,000 officials at a time. A few years ago, NASO asked former officials when and why they stopped officiating. Here are two sobering statistics:

- Eighty percent of new officials stop officiating after two years.
- Among all officials who stop officiating, seventy-five percent said that they stopped because of *the behavior of adults*.

Let's use some real numbers for just a second to understand the impact of these statistics. If a state manages to recruit one hundred new officials this year, only twenty of them will still be officiating in year three. Of the eighty who stop officiating, sixty will stop because of the behavior of parents, fans, and coaches.

This is a serious problem that, if ignored, will become a crisis in youth sports. I know that many people aren't particularly fond of the officials, but the fact is that the games cannot be played without them.

## How do we get more officials?

Now that we know there is a problem, we need to work on solutions to fix it. We need to work on ways that will help recruit and retain sports officials.

There are some things that can be done from the officiating side—more officials recruiting, better training for new officials, and an increase in mentoring programs for recruits, just to name a few. These are all things that I'm personally going to work on.

But the good news is that you too, as a coach, can have an impact on the recruiting and retaining of new officials so that we can put a dent in the shortage. Remember the stats above, and now consider them together with this statistic, from the same NASO survey of more than 17,000 officials:

- *Fifty-four percent of officials surveyed believe that coaches have the greatest impact on sportsmanship.*

It should be noted that coaches were the overwhelming answer to the impact on sportsmanship, with parents being next, at only twenty-three percent.

This is good news, because it means that by making a commitment to good sportsmanship and a positive relationship with officials, you can have more of a positive impact on overall sportsmanship than anyone else. And when you make a positive impact on sportsmanship and players' and coaches' relationships with officials, it means that the environment for recruiting new officials is better.

It makes sense, right? If you're putting to use the things you've learned in this book, you'll be motivating officials to want to work for you. If you're motivating existing officials to work for you, that means that they'll be motivated to recruit other officials who will want to work for you. Over time, the positive environment you're creating for yourself, your players, and the officials will attract more people who want to officiate. The good reputation you will build as a result of using the the strategies and tactics you've learned in this book will mean that when you ask someone about getting into officiating, they're more likely to take you up on it.

## We must work together

Just as coaches and officials must work together to create a positive game environment and experience, we're all going to have to work together to close the gap we have in available officials to ensure the health of our sports into the future.

I can promise you that I'm going to do my part to close that gap and recruit and train better officials.

By reading this book, you're showing that you are committed to creating the type of environment and relationships that will help recruit and retain more officials. If you put the things you've learned in this book into action, you'll be doing your part to recruit more officials by ensuring an environment that makes officials want to do their job every game, and want to do it to the best of their abilities.

Now, let's get to work—together.